THE SECRET LIFE

(A play in three acts)

&

The Heritage of the Actor

(An essay)

Harley Granville Barker
adapted by
Richard Nelson

Preface by
Richard Nelson & Colin Chambers

BROADWAY PLAY PUBLISHING INC
New York
www.broadwayplaypub.com
info@broadwayplaypub.com

THE SECRET LIFE
© adaptation copyright 2022 Richard Nelson

First edition: October 2022
I S B N: 978-0-88145-935-7

Book design: Marie Donovan
Page make-up: Adobe InDesign
Typeface: Palatino

HARLEY GRANVILLE BARKER, (1877-1946), actor, playwright, director, producer, theatre visionary; his other plays include AGNES COLANDER, THE VOYSEY INHERITANCE, WASTE, THE MADRAS HOUSE, and HIS MAJESTY. Other writings include the multi-volume *Prefaces to Shakespeare, The Exemplary Theatre*, and *A National Theatre.*

PREFACE

1.

Hardly ever performed.

> "It is a very great thing, that play of yours. I
> hate plays, because I'm no theatre-goer, & the
> unpractised form is knobby and uncouth to my wits;
> but the characters come through the writing with
> a shout. Your politicians are really politicians…
> The thing is clearly meant to be played, isn't it?" T
> E Lawrence, in a letter (1923) to Granville Barker
> about THE SECRET LIFE.

> "…the best [Barker] has written…never a word
> wasted." George Moore in his *Conversations in Ebury
> Street* (1924)

Again and again, over decades, various writers
returned to this play, probing its mysteries, finding
new meanings. The novelist Colin Wilson gave it a
chapter in his book, *The Outsider*, relating the main
character to those of Hemingway and Camus.

> "Man is as much a slave to his immediate
> surroundings now as he was when he lived in
> tree-huts. Give him the highest, the most exciting
> thoughts about man's place in the universe, the
> meaning of history; they can all be snuffed out in
> a moment if he wants his dinner, or feels irritated
> by a child squalling on a bus. He is bound by
> pettiness. [The play's main character] Strowde [is]

acutely sensitive to this, but not strong enough to do anything about it. "

Barker wrote THE SECRET LIFE over several years, possibly beginning in 1919, not long after the world war had ended; it was published in 1923 when his reputation as a playwright was at its pinnacle. The foremost drama critic of his day, William Archer, had recently written:

> "[Granville Barker] stands, in my eyes, second to none of his contemporaries... I do not hesitate to say that I consider [his] plays the biggest things our modern movement has produced." [1]

Barker, who died in 1946, never saw THE SECRET LIFE produced. Since then, this play has had one production in a small theater in England, and one at the Shaw Festival in Canada; and none in the United States.

Numerous efforts were made: the American producer Gilbert Miller optioned THE SECRET LIFE in 1922, but never produced it. In 1926, Eva Le Gallienne and her Civic Rep of New York announced in *The New York Times* THE SECRET LIFE for its coming season. But a production never happened. And so the play, which Barker's first biographer, in the mid-1950s, called "one of the most beautifully written plays of the present century," [2] remains unproduced in the United States and virtually unknown everywhere else.

Today we publish THE SECRET LIFE together with Granville Barker's seminal essay, *The Heritage of the*

---

[1]   William Archer, *Old Drama and the New: An Essay in Re-Valuation* (London: Heinemann, 1923), p. 129
[2]   C P Purdom, *Harley Granville Barker: Man of the Theatre, Dramatist and Scholar* (London: Rockliff, 1955), p. 202.

Actor. Barker wrote the two at the same time with the hope of publishing them together in one volume; but for some unknown reason they never were. The two works, play and essay, are deeply connected, each illuminates the other.

2.

Doing and Being.

The Heritage of the Actor, first published in *The Quarterly Review* (1923), was a revelatory essay about the art of acting; in it Barker argues for a new style of performing, one that the 'modern theatre' is uniquely able to explore.

"What…is the actor's case; what should he claim from the modern drama; what has he to offer? There was more need, as well as more scope, for physical action upon the older stage, even as there was for the spell-binding sway of verse. But now the attention of an audience can be focused upon the smallest details without either words or action being used to mark them, light, darkness, and silence can be made eloquent in themselves, a whole gamut of effectiveness has been added. It has brought new obligations—of accuracy, of sincerity, of verisimilitude in general, as we have noted. Then gain and loss both must be reflected in the actor's opportunity. His chances of doing are curtailed; in their stead new obligations of being are laid upon him. Can he not turn them to his profit?"

In its essence, Barker preaches in this essay, the art of acting is being and not doing.

Barker first witnessed this possibility (though he had been groping towards it for much of his career) when he visited the Moscow Art Theatre in 1914.

"It was when I saw the Moscow people interpreting Chekhov that I fully realized what I had been struggling towards—and that I saw how much actors could add to a play." [3]

"I saw *The Three Sisters* and *The Cherry Orchard.* Well, I had not believed till then that there could be perfection of achievement in the theatre. Twenty years of rough and tumble stage work in London had driven me…to accept the limitations of my trade and [forget] my dreams." [4]

What he found in Moscow was acting that seemed truthful or—in the word that Barker often used—that had verisimilitude.

"One is tempted," he wrote " to imagine a play—to be written in desperate defiance of Aristotle—from which *doing* would be eliminated altogether, in which nothing but *being* would be left. The task set the actors of it would be to interest their audience in what the characters were, quite apart from anything they might do; to set up, that is to say, the relation by which all important human intimacies exist. If the art of the theatre could achieve this it would stand alone in a great achievement."

The Heritage of the Actor is Granville Barker's effort at describing this new art of acting. And THE SECRET LIFE is the play he wrote for actors trained in this way.

The conflict between 'being' and 'doing' of course is more than the basis for a new acting style or even of an artistic aesthetic; this tension carries with it a world view; that is one where our true selves—our, let's call it , verisimilitude, the truth of oneself—lies not in what

[3]   Letter from Barker to William Archer, Oct. 1, 1923.
[4]   Barker, *At the Moscow Art Theatre, Manchester Guardian,* July 7, 1917.

we do, but in who or what we are. What we don't say
or do, what we often hide, and what is outside of our
conscious control—that is our secret self or our secret
life.

How one views this secret life, or how one attempts
to view it, lies at the heart of both this play and this
essay, which is a road map for how to approach a
performance of the play.

Much as absurdist theater evolved as a reaction to
the horrors of World War II, THE SECRET LIFE is in
part a response to the aftermath of WWI; the bloodiest
war (until then) in humanity's history, and one which
seemed to have little justification, or reason. Something
wicked had 'burst out' of civilized Europe, something
unfathomable and monstrous which had lain hidden
and secret within us.

The play, however, strives to be more than a post-war
play. And THE SECRET LIFE goes well beyond the
simple post-war notion that there is a 'beast' within us.
Barker's 'secret life' is far more complex than this. It
holds not only potential violence, but almost profound
calm—and love. And it points towards a spiritual sense
of one's self, wherein one simply is.

In a letter to T E Lawrence about the play, Barker
wrote:

> "And as for your feelings about what's done: well,
> I suppose your religious biologist would say that
> this whole world has been built up on a series of
> well-intentioned mistakes; it being the intention that
> persists and survives. For further insight into which
> consideration see Act III Sc. 2." [5]

[5]   Letter from Barker to Lawrence, June 12, 1923.

Here we find the heart of Barker's play, Act III Sc. 2 [Act III Sc. 3 in our version]. We are in a white room in a house amidst snow-covered New England where an elderly retired American professor, Mr Kittredge, comforts the dying Joan:

"There is an Eastern prayer… for those who leave life behind…begins: 'From the need to know by name or by form…deliver me."

Giving oneself up to something greater, even unknowable, when that something else is perhaps neither God or a faith, but rather one's own hidden or secret self—this is the conflict of this profound and moving play.

In performance, as the essay argues, the actor needs to be open to his or her own self, and of course vulnerable, meaning not controlling or 'showing' or 'doing' one's character. The true character lies in what can't be controlled, can't be 'shown', in what—is.

The ambition is for the audience to feel this; that they are in a room with real human beings with secret lives which they do not and cannot control; where any and all 'efforts' to act or to hide or deny or overcome the complex, the complicated, and contradictory secret lives of each character is doomed. This is a profoundly rich and complex play.

The story of the play is simple: post WWI—a couple who had once been in love meet again years later; he had been an up-and-coming politician, a life he's given up; she settled into a 'respectable' life as wife and mother. When the play begins, she has lost her children in the war, her house has burned in a fire and by the end of the first act, she has lost her husband as well. The couple struggle to come together again—to 'make something', to do something. He plans to return to politics, and everyone believes they will get married.

But she backs away, feeling that this 'effort' isn't right. She flees to America—on her way to Japan—seeking some peace and understanding. By the end, ill with cancer, she dreams of bygone places:

"Yesterday I was in camp again beyond Khartoum… watching the little black babies crawl about the sand. I can remember one that died, and didn't want to die… most of them, you know, come and go as easily…and he fought the air with his fists."

In a hopeless time, amidst unfathomable tragedy and savagery, we fight the air with our fists.

This beautiful (perhaps Barker's most beautiful) play is also mysterious, and equal to Ibsen's great late plays. ("The later Ibsen is my master." [6]) It would simplify to say it is but a response to the devastation of an awful war; though of course that sense of loss is in the air. The play is about something more. It is about who and what we are; what is hidden and unseen, and all that we cannot control. It is about the savagery inside us, as well as the love and peace that are within us all.

Barker gives an interesting clue in the play's opening moments as an unseen man comes to the end of 'a curious, half sung, half spoken, performance of *Tristan and Isolde*'. It is a clue that is both universal and very personal. *Tristan* universally is known as one of art's greatest expression of pure love. And this particular opera was one Barker and his second wife, Helen, saw together in 1915 in New York as they fell in love.

This play and the theory of acting articulated in the essay have a spiritual quality, portraying the unfathomable beasts inside us, which sit side by side with unfathomable love and inner peace.

[6]   Letter from Barker to Wm. Archer, Oct. 1, 1923.

Granville Barker is well known to be one of the twentieth century's greatest directors and Shakespeare scholars, and as such he has influenced and continues to influence generations of theater artists and theater productions. THE SECRET LIFE is the high point of his distinguished playwriting career—a career that, in our minds at least, has almost no equal in the modern English-language theater.
-—R Nelson & C Chambers

Why this revision?

"I never have—I cannot—write an unactable play: it would be against nature, against second nature anyhow: I act it as I write it. But there is no English company of actors so trained to interpret thought and the less crude emotions…" [About THE SECRET LIFE.][7]

Granville Barker was a consummate rewriter of his plays; during his life he revised all of his major plays for subsequent productions. These revisions often involved 'thinning' out his sometimes overly complex dialogue, as well as cuts and additions. He was a man of the theater, and would be the first to admit that one often needs to adapt for production.

Following his lead, and hoping to encourage productions of this important play, I have 'thinned' out, for clarity's sake, some of the dialogue and made cuts. And I have made one significant change: Act III is reordered. What was formerly Act III sc. 3 is now Act III sc. 2, and the former scene 2, is now scene 3 and the end of the play. I did this with some encouragement by Barker himself:

[7]   Letter from Barker to Wm. Archer, Sept. 22, 1923.

"Act III is weak…" he wrote, " I tried and tried to complete it, but couldn't." [8]

Otherwise, the play is as written and as published in 1923; now given here in the hope of furthering new productions, perhaps even its American premiere.

"Such plays as The Secret Life…may serve, if only by example, to set actors new problems and to widen the theatre's appeal. It needs widening." [9]

—R Nelson

---

[8]   Letter from Barker to Wm. Archer, Sept. 28, 1923.
[9]   Letter from Barker to St. John Ervine, Oct. 2, 1923.

THE SECRET LIFE
A Play in Three Acts
(1919-1922)
Harley Granville Barker
Adapted by Richard Nelson

CHARACTERS & SETTING

EVAN STROWDE, *a one-time politician, nearly 50.*
ELEANOR STROWDE, *his sister, a few years older.*
OLIVER GAUNTLETT, *his illegitimate son, 25. Wounded in the war.*
JOAN WESTBURY, *early 40s.*
MILDRED, COUNTESS OF PECKHAM, OLIVER'*s mother and* EVAN'*s one-time lover.*
DOROTHY GAUNTLETT, *her daughter.*
STEPHEN SEROCOLD, *a politician and the* COUNTESS' *brother.*

American visitors:

MR KITTREDGE, *a retired professor.*
SUSAN, *his granddaughter.*

Politicians (Can be played by the same actor):

SIR GEOFFREY SALOMONS
SIR LESLIE HERIOT
LORD CLUMBERMERE

The first ACT takes place at a seaside cottage in August; the second at Braxted Abbey, the country house of the Serocords; in the following June; the third in EVAN'*s home in London, and at Countesbury, Massachusetts, in the March following that.*

ACT ONE

Scene One

(August. A house that faces the sea; steps that lead up to the loggia. A warm summer night; the piano has been moved out to the loggia; around which are gathered four or five people. Because of the parapet, that bounds the loggia, they cannot be seen. But their voices can be plainly heard, and one of the party—a man—is coming to the end of a curious, half-sung, half-spoken performance of Tristan and Isolde. *He accompanies himself on the piano. He proceeds in English when it happens to fit the music, when it doesn't he relapses into the German. On the white steps sits a solitary figure in white;* JOAN WESTBURY.)

STEPHEN: *(Off)* …weherndern all! And sinking… be drinking…unbewusst…hochste Lust! Uplifted, transfigured, Isolde sinks into Brangaene's arms. Hush! Her spirit is passing. The faithful Brangaene relaxes her hold of the lifeless body…

SALOMONS: *(Off)* Always an awkward moment!

STEPHEN: *(Off)* Shut up! Awestruck in death's presence the rough soldiers stand motionless.

EVAN: *(Off)* Their hard eyes fill with tears.

STEPHEN: *(Off, protesting violently through the harmonies)* No!

EVAN: *(Off)* You used to fill them with tears.

STEPHEN: *(Off)* Never! King Mark, stern and noble, calm without though inwardly shaken…

EVAN: *(Off)* Wagner always must be flattering that sort of man.

SALOMONS: *(Off)* Everyone does.

STEPHEN: *(Off, drowning them with voice and piano both)* …raises his hand as if in benediction of the traffic lovers. The twilight deepens. The curtain falls.

(STEPHEN closes with some elaboration. There is, however, no applause; an ironic silence rather. After a moment, MISS ELEANOR STROWDE'S *voice is heard, saying…)*

ELEANOR: *(Off)* Thank you.

STEPHEN: *(Off)* Not so bad, considering! May I have a drink?

ELEANOR: *(Off)* They'll be in the dining room, Evan.

(EVAN stands and is seen unhurriedly walking across to the dining room and turns on the light there.)

STEPHEN: *(Off)* Sir Geoffrey Salomons, KCB, your performance of King Mark…for all that I thumped the notes for you…was rotten.

SALOMONS: *(Off)* Time has, I fear, added a patine to my voice.

STEPHEN: *(Of)* Patina, Sir. And in the future I shall address your envelopes KCB flat.

EVAN: *(Off, calling back)* What about my Kurwenal?

STEPHEN: *(Off)* What indeed.

SALOMONS: *(Off)* You have been shamelessly practicing, Serocold.

STEPHEN: *(Off)* Certainly…I gave half a morning to it. Tristan, Isolde, chorus and orchestra…Eleanor's note telling me you'd be dining…and that very day I'd happened on my old score.

SALOMONS: *(Off)* Which I notice has my name on it.

STEPHEN: *(Off)* Horrid habit it was of yours…writing your name in other people's books. *(He forces a sigh, the mocking sigh of reminiscent middle-age)* Well, I shall never make that noise again!

(EVAN's head appears again.)

EVAN: Whiskey, Stephen?

STEPHEN: *(Off)* Not much.

SALOMONS: *(Off)* I've been trying to recall our last bout.

STEPHEN: *(Off)* I came back to Balliol in the spring after Evan got his fellowship.

SALOMONS: *(Off)* I was down by then.

STEPHEN: *(Off)* You were there.

EVAN: Soda?

STEPHEN: *(Off)* Tap.

EVAN: Same for you, Geoffrey?

SALOMONS: *(Off)* Soda. No whisky.

(He heads off to the living room again.)

ELEANOR: *(Off)* The water looks worse than it tastes. But we have to bring every drinkable drop from the village.

STEPHEN: *(Off)* I suppose one can't sink a well so near the sea.

SALOMONS: *(Off, with the slightest touch of orientalism)* But it's a charming place, Miss Strowde.

ELEANOR: *(Off)* For a summer six weeks. Evan likes the bathing.

(EVAN returning with the drinks notices the still figure on the steps. He is a man of fifty. LADY WESTBURY [JOAN] is rather younger. A woman that, in her youth, must have been

very flower-like; the fragility, and a sense of fragrance about her, remains.)

EVAN: Is that you, Joan?

JOAN: Yes.

EVAN: Could you endure it?

JOAN: I could hear perfectly. Look at the moon.

EVAN: It might be a ship on fire.

JOAN: Burnt out.

ELEANOR: *(Off)* My dear…I thought you'd stolen to bed. Don't sit there without something round your shoulders. You're not in Egypt now.

JOAN: The desert's far colder.

ELEANOR: I shall get you a shawl.

JOAN: No, Eleanor.

ELEANOR: *(Off)* And an ugly one…as a punishment.

(She stands, and her head is visible as she heads into the living room.)

(STEPHEN SEROCOLD now leans over the loggia; a middle-aged man, who has kept his youth.)

STEPHEN: I fear we made a horrid noise.

JOAN: I always come home hungry for music.

SALOMONS: *(Off)* A horrid sight, Serocold.

STEPHEN: What is?

(SIR GEOFFREY SALOMONS stands and joins him.)

SALOMONS: Romantic youth…dragged from its grave and gibbeted. The three of us used to meet in my rooms at Oxford, Lady Westbury…I had the piano, that's why they put up with me. Tristan was the great dish…served as it has just been served to you. And

I've known us sit silent for an hour after…gorged with emotion.

(EVAN, *having given* STEPHEN *his whiskey, asks* JOAN…)

EVAN: Whiskey, lemonade, or Eleanor's butter-milk?

JOAN: Nothing, thank you.

SALOMONS: If you had but stuck to art and your ideals, my good Serocold, you might now be worth three pounds a week as a pianist in a cinema.

STEPHEN: And a steadier, better-paid job on the balance, it'd be, than my present one.

SALOMONS: I thought you were a venal politician. I have always envied you.

STEPHEN: No one will bribe me, Salomons…no one, at least, has ever tried. And my beauty's faded in my country's service…late hours in the House are ruinous to my complexion…

(ELEANOR *comes down the stairs with the shawl for* JOAN. *She is grey-haired; a few years older than her brother.*)

ELEANOR: Put this on.

(*She wraps it round her with a certain austere tenderness.*)

JOAN: It's not ugly.

ELEANOR: Not on you.

JOAN: Thank you, kind Eleanor…

SALOMONS: We sit here and celebrate with due mockery our emancipation from the toils of the wanton art that seduced our youth. Join us, Miss Strowde.

ELEANOR: I? Why?

SALOMONS: For one thing…you wouldn't be so down as you were at dinner on poor Serocold's political morality.

STEPHEN: My political immorality.

SALOMONS: My dear Serocold, persuade Evan and
Eleanor that it's we who are poor without them.

ELEANOR: We must all cash in our principles, must we?

SALOMONS: Not for mere cash.

EVAN: Stephen wants to buy me back. But I protest
there's nothing left of me to sell.

STEPHEN: Nonsense.

EVAN: Not one principle. I have left the marketplace.
And when I hear you talk politics nowawdays,
Stephen, it's like hearing you sing Tristan.

STEPHEN: As bad as that.

EVAN: As incredible. Scratch off our clothes, O survivor
of wrecked civilisations, and instead of the savage it's
likelier you'll find nothing at all.

SALOMONS: But, my dear good heroic fellow…why not
be content with appearances? Why risk disillusion?
The achievement in a hundred thousand years or
so of the gentleman, the lady, and the leisure class
with appetites turned to taste, is a most important
one. Don't let democratic cant belittle that. Indulge
yourselves, incidentally, in a little art…a few good
tunes, a picture or so, a scene full of pretty girls.
Provide such things…for now that the human brute is
well fed, his passions need distracting…

EVAN: And a little alcohol.

SALOMONS: Yes, if you can't be sentimental without
it. But never be carried off on crusades you can't
finance… Don't overdraw on your moral credit.
Don't, for one moment, let art or religion or patriotism
persuade you that you mean more than you do. I must
be off.

ELEANOR: Before you're answered.

SALOMONS: Answers are echoes.

ELEANOR: What does that mean?

STEPHEN: It means that we all talk the same nonsense and all have to do the next thing there is to be done.

SALOMONS: But thank you for a charming evening.

ELEANOR: Till October.

SALOMONS: The Committee is to meet on the fifteenth. But you'll get your summons.

ELEANOR: My first full-fledged official committee. I feel cock-a-hoop.

(*A skittish phrase for* ELEANOR. STEPHEN *goes back to the piano to strum delicately and sing little snatches. 'Tristan,' 'Isolde.'*)

SALOMONS: Good-bye, Lady Westbury. Once more, my condolences upon the catastrophe. But I must not agree that insurance is a mockery.

JOAN: My first fire! It's inspiriting to have to start life again in one's dressing-gown and the gardener's boots.

EVAN: Your car's round here, Geoffrey.

SALOMONS: Good-night, Serocold.

(STEPHEN *sings to the melody of the Liebstod.*)

STEPHEN: (*Off*) Good-night, Sir Geoffrey…Salomons KCB flat…hidden handed bureaucrat…

SALOMONS: (*Heading down the stairs*) Not going abroad?

EVAN: (*Walking with* SALOMONS) I've no impulse to. Europe still reproaches me. Perhaps…in the winter.

SALOMONS: If Serocold don't recapture you.

(*They have gone down the steps and away round the house,* EVAN *kindling a pocket torch. The two women lean together on the parapet.*)

JOAN: You've never been to Karnak, Eleanor?

ELEANOR: No.

JOAN: We break our journey at Luxor whenever there's time. You should stand on the great gate and watch the moon rising over the Nile…and then think of all the armies that have marched…

ELEANOR: *(Touching her hand)* My child, you're as cold as a toad. Cheer up! Mark'll be home for good next year…and think of the fun you'll have re-building.

JOAN: *(With a rather wan smile)* Energetic Eleanor! But as if he hadn't enough to worry him in Cairo at this moment.

ELEANOR: *(The kindly scold)* You go to bed now.

STEPHEN: *(Off, as he softly strums)* How many more volumes to this infernal history that Evan has found refuge in?

ELEANOR: One to publish…one to write.

STEPHEN: *(Off)* How long'll that take you?

ELEANOR: I don't know.

STEPHEN: *(Off)* Can't you finish it for him, Eleanor?

ELEANOR: Hardly.

STEPHEN: *(Off)* Books must be written, I admit…but there are lots of men fit for nothing else. We philistine politicians may be a poor lot…but we do get things done.

JOAN: *(Half to herself, looking at the moon and the sea)* I must pray now to the moon…as one burnt-out lady to another…. To teach me to order my ways.

(STEPHEN *breaks into song again; from the Second Act this time.)*

STEPHEN: *(Off)* Oh rest upon us…night du Liebe.

JOAN: Burnt out inside…the moon is. Gutted…such an ugly word!

STEPHEN: *(Off, singing away)* Give forgetting…that I live. Take me out…in deinen schuss…

(ELEANOR has gone into the sitting room. JOAN stares out to sea.)

(End of Scene)

Scene Two

(Morning, the sun is shining. ELEANOR, wrapped in a fur coat, is sitting in the loggia, writing. STEPHEN, dressed for his journey, comes out of the house and stands by the head of the steps talking to her [unseen].)

STEPHEN: Good morning, ma'am.

ELEANOR: *(Off)* Has the car come?

STEPHEN: Not yet, I think. I'm interrupting?

ELEANOR: *(Off)* No, I've just finished.

STEPHEN: Proofs?

ELEANOR: *(Off)* Pages one to sixty…volume four…of the infernal history.

STEPHEN: We've been in for a swim. I left Evan basking. Are you cold?

ELEANOR: *(Off)* I work in a fur coat all the year round. Thin blood…old age.

STEPHEN: Intellectual passion, Eleanor…chilling but admirable. Am I to post these in London?

(She stands, her head now visble above the parapet.)

ELEANOR: I'm coming up with you…for the day.

STEPHEN: Eighty miles up and eighty miles down at eighty in the shade.

ELEANOR: I'm going to lunch at Kate Gossett's to meet Lord Clumbermere.

STEPHEN: And what does Kate want with him?

ELEANOR: I want fifty thousand pounds out of him for the Institute of Social Service.

STEPHEN: Well…I daresay you'll get it.

ELEANOR: I'm told he's a good little man.

STEPHEN: He's good for that much.

ELEANOR: *(Pointedly)* You should know.

STEPHEN: I assure you, we got nothing for his peerage. Reward of merit! I did hope he'd be substantially grateful. But devil a threepenny bit!

ELEANOR: He bought his baronetcy surely.

STEPHEN: Egerton gave him that. *(Looks back toward the house and lifts his voice a little)* Good morning, fair lady!

ELEANOR: I hope the taxi-man didn't hurry you. How's Lester?

(JOAN, to whom this has been spoken, comes from the sitting room, and speaks first to ELEANOR, then to STEPHEN.)

JOAN: She had a good night. My heroic maid who went back for my pearls.

STEPHEN: Her point of honour.

ELEANOR: She didn't get them.

JOAN: I'm almost glad she didn't. Pearls at that price! *(To Eleanor)* You saw her arm. We discuss now what we'll do with the insurance money. She's to decide.

(She goes back into the house; a moment later comes out again with a parasol, goes down the steps and sits on one of the benches there silently. ELEANOR being now quite free of her writing table, STEPHEN fixes her.)

STEPHEN: You may take it from me, Eleanor, that the pro-Leaguers will vote against Egerton on the Japanese question…and he'll resign…and Bellingham must be sent for. He can form a government even without dissolving. And I'll lay you five to two that it all comes off before Christmas.

(ELEANOR *lets* STEPHEN *finish; then she shakes her head with a half smile.*)

ELEANOR: I'm not interested, Stephen.

STEPHEN: You definitely refuse to help shepherd Evan back into the fold.

ELEANOR: I'm sorry your week-end has been wasted.

STEPHEN: I've enjoyed myself. Don't be nasty.

ELEANOR: If Evan chooses to go back into politics he will, whatever I say.

STEPHEN: And of course he will… It's the obvious thing to do.

ELEANOR: If he ever serves under Mr Bellingham again…I shall be surprised.

STEPHEN: You must serve under the man who's there. Bellingham has his failings…. And his wife's a disaster.

ELEANOR: I don't call Mrs Bellingham a disaster.

STEPHEN: She's so dull.

ELEANOR: My objection to your respected chief is simply that he's a liar.

STEPHEN: I shouldn't call him a liar.

ELEANOR: …That he's a trickster.

STEPHEN: He can be tricky when he's driven to it.

ELEANOR: He has no principles.

STEPHEN: *(Cheerily)* I tell him that too.

ELEANOR: He is constantly disloyal to his friends.

STEPHEN: No, Eleanor, there you're wrong. And it hurts him when they say the sort of things about him that

you're saying. But how can he go on working with
them afterwards?

ELEANOR: Would you tolerate a tithe of his dishonesty
in your own lawyer?

STEPHEN: Ah…that opens a wide question. I want
an honest lawyer. I've got one I think…and I do my
best to deserve him. I'm a good democrat. I'll work
with any one who'll work with me. And I say that
the great thing is to keep things going…to make for
righteousness somehow…by the line of least resistance.

ELEANOR: You've all deteriorated since the war.

STEPHEN: And what sort of a morality's yours, may I
ask…truckling to Clumbermere for money? Travelling
up to London to do it, too.

ELEANOR: I offer Lord Clumbermere social salvation….
Cheap at the price. I've nothing else to sell him. We
must start. Have I got a hat on? Joan, dear, forgive me
deserting you. Be nice to Evan. I'll be back to dinner…

STEPHEN: With fifty thousand honest sovereigns
jingling in your pocket!

ELEANOR: You'll find me in the car…in two minutes.

(ELEANOR *goes into the house.* STEPHEN *comes down a
few steps and leans against the wall within a good range of*
JOAN.)

STEPHEN: We physicians of the body politic, you'll
observe…of whatever school, are at one in our firm
faith in bleeding.

JOAN: Who is Lord Clumbermere…ought I to know?

STEPHEN: Tanner's Inks he was. God knows what
else now…now that he himself is appropriately de-
personalised into Clumbermere. An able devil.

JOAN: You want Evan back.

STEPHEN: Bellingham wants to make it up with him. But Evan must hold out a hand.

JOAN: Was he trying to work with?

STEPHEN: Infinitely.

JOAN: But you keep on trying.

STEPHEN: It's my job.

JOAN: D'you think Eleanor's is the right woman's way into politics?

STEPHEN: I don't like women in public affairs, I'm afraid…though it's too unpopular a thing to say. They make the bad worse…not better.

JOAN: Her Institute and her Guilds.

STEPHEN: They're nice new toys.

JOAN: And Sir Geoffrey's Committee! She thinks you'll soon be left chattering in your clubs.

STEPHEN: She has been devilling for Evan all her life. She's sick of it…that's all.

JOAN: You miss Mary. *(After a moment)* I'm so glad I was home that summer and saw her…

STEPHEN: She was very fond of you.

JOAN: Life's eddies are so strange. Evan and Eleanor take this cottage in August…I'm burnt out of house and home, and cast on their mercy.

STEPHEN: And do you remember our first meeting?

JOAN: Shamelessly…no.

STEPHEN: Evan and Eleanor, Mary and I, you and your husband…emptied together from various trains on the platform at Verona.

JOAN: I was on my honeymoon.

STEPHEN: I had a vision of it this morning…as I floated on the sea. And of the man with the guitar who offered to pass the time for us by singing 'Rigoletto' right through for three lire. My Tristan fooleries must have reminded me. And our last meeting?

JOAN: Such is the blank I call my mind…

STEPHEN: Tea at the Military Tournament…nineteen thirteen. Your boy was with you.

JOAN: Which?

STEPHEN: The one that was killed.

JOAN: Which? They were both killed.

STEPHEN: Both?

JOAN: Within a month.

STEPHEN: *(There being nothing better to say)* I forgot. I won't blunder further by saying sympathetic things. I fear I used sometimes, rather meanly, to thank God Mary and I had no children. Then I lost her.

JOAN: *(Detaching her mind)* I was once taken through Vicker's to see the armour-plate making…and the big steam hammer cracked a nut for my benefit. They gave me the nut, and told me just where to place it. Mighty goings on leave us, don't you think, too dazed to complain? Won't Eleanor be waiting for you?

STEPHEN: Heavens…yes. Good-bye.

JOAN: Good-bye.

STEPHEN: Come and see Braxted again some day?

JOAN: I'd like to.

(STEPHEN goes into the house and so away. JOAN sits looking out to sea. After a moment, EVAN, in a bathing suit covered by a dressing-down, comes as if from the beach. She, motionless, is aware of him.)

JOAN: Good morning.

EVAN: Did you sleep?

JOAN: Yes.

EVAN: The night through?

JOAN: Oh no.

EVAN: For how long?

JOAN: Three hours. Don't give me away.

EVAN: I'll give you till Wednesday to get a night's rest. Then I'll tell on you.

JOAN: I don't want to be doctored. I'm having such a peaceful time.

EVAN: Eleanor gone?

JOAN: With Stephen Serocold.

EVAN: We've a day together.

JOAN: *(Not indifferently)* Yes.

EVAN: Our first for a while.

JOAN: For a long time. You're to go back into Parliament, please, Evan, and into the Cabinet…at once.

EVAN: The voice of Stephen?

JOAN: Why don't you?

EVAN: I must dress.

JOAN: Don't you believe in yourself any longer?

EVAN: Is that enough of a faith? I've been clearing out the wardrobe of my mind lately. I used to have quite a fashionable mind. I find worn-out stuff and stuff I've never worn. And one can't get rid of it. It mocks me from the rubbish heap.

JOAN: Better to be burnt out.

EVAN: Yes…you're lucky.

JOAN: I do feel, though, that one cannot start in collecting again. Let God's eye behold me still in my dressing-gown and gardener's boots.

EVAN: Shall we lunch out here? It won't be too hot. The parlourmaid's eye not being as God's, I will shift to a less symbolical attire…

(EVAN *goes in to dress.* JOAN *does not move.*)

(*End of Scene*)

Scene 3

(*It is nearly midnight, and the moon is shining.* JOAN, *wrapped from the chill in a white cloak, is sitting on the steps as before.* EVAN *comes out of the house.*)

JOAN: What had happened? Is she very tired?

EVAN: She hasn't come. He drove here to tell me.

JOAN: But it's the last train.

EVAN: No. …I've sent him to the Junction now. There's a nine-thirty express she might have caught.

JOAN: And if not?

EVAN: She could motor forty miles and get here about three in the morning.

JOAN: Couldn't she have telegraphed?

EVAN: Yes…up to seven.

JOAN: Not like Eleanor.

EVAN: She'll come.

JOAN: Is she still rifling Lord What's-his-name's pockets…while Kate Gossett holds him down? The silly man must have been struggling.

(*By this,* EVAN *and* JOAN *have settled themselves to wait.*)

JOAN: A long day, Evan.

EVAN: Has it seemed so?

JOAN: I believe I've told you everything. You've not told me much.

EVAN: Several anecdotes. Do you want more? I've a good memory. Sometimes I exercise it to see if the anecdotes strung together have any meaning.

JOAN: Ought I to be ashamed to have so little to tell? No spiritual adventures. Housekeeping in odd corners of the world…a husband and two children.

EVAN: Dutiful happiness.

JOAN: Yes.

EVAN: As we agreed then…all for the best.

JOAN: I've never doubted it.

EVAN: The love for Mark survived. And you had your boys.

JOAN: I couldn't have lived my love for you, Evan…it would have killed me.

EVAN: Did I understand that? *(Nearly laughs)* It's always hard to believe that a little human happiness will hurt one.

JOAN: *(Continuing)* It's shocking for a woman to discover that wifehood and motherhood are really best carried through as matters of business…and that if she loves a man she can only make him miserable.

EVAN: I'd be glad enough to be made unhappy once again. And I can be less of an altruist…than I was then.

JOAN: *(With a touch of mischief)* Has no one managed it in these eighteen years? No, no…I'm not curious.

(EVAN *faces* JOAN, *and asks very seriously, but almost disinterestedly:)*

EVAN: In the sense that you've always loved me…do you love me still?

JOAN: *(Nods)* I keep it a secret from my everyday self.

(A short pause)

EVAN: *(Breaking the tension)* Still, you've not much to complain of. Mark's a first-rate fellow.

(JOAN's voice is never hard, nor ever dry, but sometimes it empties of all tone; as now:)

JOAN: My boys are gone.

EVAN: I won't pretend to understand what that means.

JOAN: One's capable, you know, of uncomprehended suffering. I watched women making a sort of emotional profit out of their loss. People called me stoical…but it was only that I didn't understand…or want to. Why ask what an earthquake's for? My bitterest moment was when I came home to find their kit sent back from France. Burnt up with everything else now, I'm glad to think. The emptyings, poor dears, of their pockets… of a dead boy's pockets. The night the second news had come we lay awake holding hands…and Mark said suddenly: "I'm sorry, my…I'm sorry." And I said: "Oh, Mark, don't apologise." *(She comes back with relief to practical things.)* I wish I'd not left him just now…but the doctor won't let me stay out the summer there. His work's a failure, he says…so they thought they must send him red ribbons and things. When his KCB badge came he threw it into the corner and cursed. It has been a bad three years. We used to fear that you and your party would come in to theorise us out of existence. I remember the evening when he brought the paper to Gizeh with the news of your bye-election majority. "Evan will take three steps into the F O," he said… "and I shall resign." *(A little grimly)* It's his friends have let him down.

EVAN: Did he really picture me astraddle before the official mantelpiece with my chest puffed out and: Gentlemen, now I'm in power…?

JOAN: But why aren't you, Evan?

(Pause)

EVAN: If I say: Thanks to you…don't misunderstand…

JOAN: *(Puzzled)* Oh, my dear…

EVAN: But understand I do thank you that I am not a popular political figure today…putting on all the airs of wisdom.

JOAN: Was your history writing the better choice?

EVAN: Well, the Industrial History is honestly labored stuff. You've not read it?

JOAN: Horrid confession…no. I began to.

EVAN: More shameful still.

JOAN: Three volumes.

EVAN: And a fourth to come.

JOAN: And a fifth.

EVAN: Perhaps. A job almost any one could have done, and nobody did. Shall I tell you why I took it on…even before the other job failed me?

JOAN: Why?

EVAN: This sounds unselfish…it wasn't. I really had to find something more than housekeeping for Eleanor to do. My 'marriage'.

JOAN: It's been a happy one?

EVAN: Quite.

JOAN: What's to happen when the history is finished?

EVAN: *(Businesslike)* Committees are seeking her out. Even Salomons, you see, that shrewd appraiser of what's worth while...

JOAN: I meant—to you?

EVAN: Eleanor, grown a power in the land and backed by much Clumbermere money, may find me employment.

JOAN: *(Ignoring that)* When will the last volume be done?

(EVAN *turns his head suddenly.*)

EVAN: I hear the car changing gear on Pewsey Hill.

JOAN: He has been very quick.

EVAN: Impossibly. She'll have found a taxi at the Junction, and they've met half-way.

JOAN: Evan...stir yourself out of this hopelessness and disbelief.

EVAN: When the donkey's at the end of his tether and has eaten his patch bare, he's to cut capers and kick up a dust, is he?

JOAN: Have you no purpose left in you? Don't you want to be a power in the world?

EVAN: Save me from the illusion of power. I once had a glimpse...and I thank you for it, my dear...of a power that is in me. But that won't answer to any call.

JOAN: Not to a good cause?

EVAN: Excellent causes abound. They are served...as they are...by eminent prigs making a fine parade, by little minds watching for what's to happen next. Track such men down...past picture-paper privacy, and their servants' knowledge of them. Oh, never mind if they drink a little, if they're foolish over women or sordid about money...we won't damn them for these weaknesses. But praise them for their strengths—which spring from the secret life...and what is that, but the old ignorant savagery? Nothing to be ashamed of...but why deck it with new names? Women should know, even if we forget, what savages men still are. And then there's the unbelieving mob who cry: Do something, anything, no matter what...do you devilmost...all's well while the wheels go round...while something's being done! Because if we stop to question, barbarous poverty will overwhelm us again. Are we so few steps upward from the beast that gluts and starves? *(Pause)* I'm not the first man who has found beliefs that he can't put in his pocket like so much small change. If I could be...call it in love again...then, perhaps I'd dare stretch out my hand for power.

JOAN: Don't waste time...next time...over a woman.

EVAN: I promise.

JOAN: *(Breaking the tension)* I never put such fantastic value on myself.

EVAN: Tell me how to forget you...and the meaning of you.

JOAN: I'm changed.

EVAN: You outface the years very beautifully.

JOAN: Thank you...says my vanity.

EVAN: But such things are tokens for strangers to know you by. What shines for me is the vision of the truth of you which you gave me when you said...weighing your words, I remember...when you said that you loved me.

JOAN: If I'm to stand to you for ever as a symbol of denial...of uselessness... Evan, no recording angel will consent to write: He could not be a conquering hero all for thinking of a love affair. We did wisely.

EVAN: We did right.

JOAN: No, I don't say so. I did what I felt then I could be sure of doing well… *(Short pause)* Mark says the most pitiful thing he meets is the well-meaning man who daren't stop. He sees him, he says, poor dear, in the mirror every morning.

EVAN: I'd see an ill-meaning man.

JOAN: Why?

EVAN: Can you think of a greater driving force for evil than the man who has seen a better way and accepts the worse…who knows there's a wisdom that escapes and must deny it? I'd sooner trust things to fools, if the fools would take heart, than to disillusioned men.

JOAN: *(Hearing a noise)* There's Eleanor…

EVAN: *(Getting up)* Let the busy women have a try at tidying up.

JOAN: Here she is.

EVAN: Weary, but cheerful.

(EVAN goes quickly into the house. After a moment ELEANOR comes out. Weary she may but, but she does not show it much.)

ELEANOR: Dear Joan…forgive me.

JOAN: Good hunting?

ELEANOR: Good enough. Has Evan looked after you?

JOAN: Perfectly.

(EVAN returns.)

ELEANOR: You didn't get my message. But I missed even that train.

JOAN: You have a callous brother. I said you might be lying cold and stiff. He said it was unlikely.

EVAN: No one is ever anxious about Eleanor. There are sandwiches and barley-water for you.

ELEANOR: Go to bed, Joan. I didn't dream you'd sit up.

JOAN: Naughty of me. Goodnight.

(ELEANOR *kisses* JOAN, *more tenderly than, one would say, occasion demanded.*)

ELEANOR: My dear…

JOAN: I'm sure you've most intriguing things to tell Evan about Lord Blumble-Bee… Goodnight, Evan.

EVAN: Goodnight, Joan.

(JOAN *goes. There is a little pause, as if* ELEANOR *and* EVAN *were waiting for her to get out of earshot.*)

EVAN: Well, what's wrong?

ELEANOR: Mark Westbury fell down dead in his office in Cairo this morning.

EVAN: Good God.

ELEANOR: By pure chance I met Neville Hamerton at the corner of Whitehall and he told me. So I went back with him to the F O to stop them sending her a telegram. That's what kept me, of course. Shall I tell her tonight or not?

EVAN: Yes, I should.

ELEANOR: Would she take it better from you?

EVAN: Why should she?

ELEANOR: You knew Mark very well.

EVAN: Not better than you know her.

ELEANOR: It'll seem like the end of the world. Both her boys…the house burnt down…and now this.

EVAN: Mark is an immeasurable loss. But all losses are…

ELEANOR: Evan, don't be so callous.

EVAN: I am not. It will be a great shock…and a great grief…till Nature rebels and says: Die of it, or get over it.

ELEANOR: Is this how I'm to talk to Joan?

EVAN: Don't start talking at all. Tell her Mark's dead, kiss her, and come away the moment she loosens your hand.

(ELEANOR *goes into the house. He now has but to put out the lights below, lock up and go to bed.*)

(*As he does, off, from a bedroom, a woman cries out, begins to scream.*)

END OF ACT ONE

ACT TWO

Scene One.

(Braxted Abbey, STEPHEN's home. The end of the gallery, a few windows which overlook a terrace; at the end of the gallery a writing table, commanding a view of the unseen picture gallery. A small door leading down a small turret staircase.)

(The next summer; an afternoon; the window is open. STEPHEN and MILDRED, LADY PECKHAM, his sister, on the window seat. She has just arrived.)

STEPHEN: Why go to an Anarchist meeting? And if he must go, why in God's name get arrested there!

MILDRED: They didn't charge Oliver with anything.

STEPHEN: Every paper had a paragraph.

MILDRED: A fortnight ago…all forgotten. The tradition of the English gentleman, Stephen, is that he may go where he pleases and do what he likes.

STEPHEN: Talk to your son seriously.

MILDRED: Try it yourself.

STEPHEN: I have. He says Anarchy interest him.

MILDRED: Why shouldn't it?

STEPHEN: My dear sister, I'm in the Cabinet, and I'm his uncle.

MILDRED: That's not his fault.

STEPHEN: That's what *he* said. I think it most courageous and forgiving of me to ask him down here.

MILDRED: It is. *(Nodding toward the garden)* Where did Joan Westbury spring from? I've not met her for an age.

STEPHEN: She's been about.

MILDRED: You brought Evan and Eleanor down with you?

STEPHEN: Yesterday.

MILDRED: Who else is coming?

STEPHEN: The Kittredges.

MILDRED: I've seen them.

STEPHEN: We only hold eight these days.

MILDRED: Lunching to-morrow?

STEPHEN: Bellingham.

MILDRED: You stick to your point, don't you. He hates Evan.

STEPHEN: Evan despises him.

MILDRED: *(Another glance out the window)* Are those two going to?

STEPHEN: I haven't heard so. But they're walking nicely in step. It looks connubial.

MILDRED: They'd better hurry up. They're not getting younger. She'll want more children. And why not?

STEPHEN: My dear Mildred…there are other objects in marrying.

MILDRED: That's an obvious one. Why do you ask these Kittredges?

STEPHEN: I like them…and it's as well to be civil to Americans.

MILDRED: Are they rich?

STEPHEN: I'm sure they'd hate to be thought so.

MILDRED: That's very morbid. You've no right to look so young, you know, Stephen. I wasn't out of the nursery when you were born.

OLIVER: *(Off)* Hullo, darling Mother!

MILDRED: *(She waves)* Bless you, my son.

STEPHEN: I'm still pretty vexed, Mildred, about this escape of Oliver's.

MILDRED: Nothing in it.

(JOAN, EVAN *and* OLIVER GAUNTLETT *arrive, unseen, under the window.)*

MILDRED: How are you, Joan?

JOAN: *(Off)* Do you want to know?

MILDRED: I ask.

JOAN: *(Off)* I feel like flying.

STEPHEN: Door's locked inside. I'll open it. *(He goes down the turret stairs.)*

MILDRED: Hot?

JOAN: *(Off)* No.

MILDRED: Pretty frock.

JOAN: *(Off)* One I had dyed.

MILDRED: You're losing a comb.

JOAN: *(Off)* Thank you. How's London?

MILDRED: Horrid.

(OLIVER *enters up the turret stairs. he is a young man and he has lost an arm.* EVAN *follows.* OLIVER *kisses his mother.* EVAN *has a printed offical-looking paper. He will soon open it, and sit down at the writing table.)*

OLIVER: Where's Dolly?

MILDRED: Went down to the lake with Miss Susan Kittredge. Well, Evan?

EVAN: Well, Mildred?

(No greeting could be friendlier.)

OLIVER: You look very handsome, Mother.

MILDRED: Thank you kindly. How are you?

OLIVER: Kicking. Evan won't take me on.

MILDRED: Why should he?

STEPHEN: *(Off)* Mildred, come and see the Alderney bull.

MILDRED: Now?

STEPHEN: *(Off)* Yes.

MILDRED: All right.

OLIVER: Uncle Stephen!

STEPHEN: *(Off)* Hullo!

OLIVER: I positively was not drunk.

STEPHEN: *(Off)* I wish you had been.

EVAN: *(looking up from his reading)* Distressing to the nice-minded historian…to note how aggressively moral revolutionaries become.

OLIVER: New Year before last at Blair I tried to get drunk and couldn't. Nor wine nor spirits has passed my lips since. I think I'll try again.

MILDRED: Do you feel you really must?

OLIVER: Why did you give me such a queer head?

MILDRED: *(As she kisses his head goodbye)* I sometimes wish it had been an even thicker one.

OLIVER: But what about my future?

EVAN: Did the worthy Sir Charles Phillips positively throw you down the office steps?

OLIVER: He wept over me. I resigned.

MILDRED: I shall shortly have the pleasure of telling that gentleman publicly that he's a liar.

OLIVER: For saying I was frolicsomely drunk! Dear Mother, he meant that kindly.

MILDRED: Still, I shall not deny myself the pleasure. *(She goes down the stairs.)*

OLIVER: Grin through a mask and explode an idea on them...and your Phillipses show the white scuts of their minds like rabbits.

EVAN: What precise shade of red are you? Anarchy's black by the way.

OLIVER: Evan, I will tell you a secret. I was down there searching for a Chinese debating society...and I got into the wrong meeting.

EVAN: *(Seriously)* What's wrong with the City?

OLIVER: What's wrong with a mine that's on a map and a cotton-field on a balance-sheet?

EVAN: Not primitive enough?

OLIVER: Maybe. Digging potatoes might sweat all the nonsense out of me, d'you think? But I can't.

EVAN: You play an amazing game of tennis though.

OLIVER: I write a better hand than I did.

EVAN: I don't see what use I can be. If politics are your game...won't you do better attacking the citadel of the constitution from within...as you happen to have the entrée?

OLIVER: Yes...the Right Honorable Brooke Bellingham's lunching tomorrow. I might wag my tail at him and be a Cabinet Minister in no time.

EVAN: Why not?

OLIVER: There's a longer lease for the old gang in letting the youngsters in than in keeping them out, isn't there? I'm not for bombs. There's not enough difference between a dead Bellingham and a live one.

EVAN: And there's something to be said, you know, for simple and vulgar ambition.

OLIVER: They're all twitteringly afraid of you, Evan. If your name comes up at a dinner table, Uncle Stephen gets that genial—

EVAN: They flatter me.

OLIVER: You're going to stand again at the election?

EVAN: I may.

OLIVER: They think you mean to give them hell.

EVAN: I must manage to keep up the impression.

OLIVER: I want to learn what's what. I've chucked a success in the City.

EVAN: You could have given them hell there. A spectacular bankruptcy. You've a name to discredit. That's real revolution.

OLIVER: You're spoiling for a fight, you know…for all you sit there writing niggling notes on that report to Eleanor's damned Committee.

EVAN: I'd be setting you to type them.

OLIVER: I will. Until the time comes…

EVAN: And if the time never comes?

OLIVER: How long have you believed that?

EVAN: It is my firm disbelief.

OLIVER: Then why don't you shoot yourself?

EVAN: I must finish these notes.

OLIVER: I must dress.

EVAN: Dinner at eight?

OLIVER: It takes me half an hour. But you might think me over.

EVAN: Yes, I will.

OLIVER: Thank you.

(OLIVER *goes down the gallery, leaving* EVAN *to his note-making.*)

(*End of Scene*)

Scene 2

(*Half an hour later.* EVAN *has nearly reached the end of the Report and of his notes.* MILDRED *comes down the gallery.*)

MILDRED: (*Off*) You'll be late for dinner.

EVAN: No.

(MILDRED *appears:*)

MILDRED: You will. Because I want to talk to you. (*She sits.*)

EVAN: What about?

MILDRED: Oliver.

EVAN: Yes. What do you want me to do?

MILDRED: Queer his turning to you…so instinctively.

EVAN: How long since he turned fantastically minded?

MILDRED: He has been very mum with me this last year or two.

EVAN: Is it the strain of the war still?

MILDRED: I don't see why it should be. He was only three months out…got smashed…came home.

EVAN: He had three years among the stay-at-homes… growing up to it. His mind is jangled at the moment. It mayn't last.

MILDRED: He's very unhappy. I've always wondered whether sometime he ought not to be told.

EVAN: D'you think that would cheer him?

MILDRED: D'you think it's possible he knows?

EVAN: Hardly possible. What gossip there was…

MILDRED: How should we know what gossip there was?

EVAN: I suppose it's possible.

MILDRED: Don't think I'd mind telling him he's your son.

EVAN: My dear Mildred…surely it would be a piece of wanton cruelty.

MILDRED: I consider you've a right to forbid me.

EVAN: You've been seriously thinking of telling him?

MILDRED: Yes…I'm a tough old heathen…and I'm a sentimental fool. The two things go together, I suppose.

EVAN: Often.

MILDRED: Have you any feeling for Oliver?

EVAN: Honestly?...

MILDRED: Then you haven't. Why expect it? You were pretty young. We were happy for a bit. I took a sort of pride in sending you off whistling… *(She relaxes)* I remember my father, when I was fifteen, setting forth great-aunt Charlotte to me…which had to be done as she's in the history books… He said: she was a bad lot, but a good fellow.

EVAN: You have a genius, Mildred, for making things seem simple.

MILDRED: Well…I've more energy than brains. And I never could fuss about my immortal soul. I'm not sure that I have one. I used to think I might grow one. But if you can only get it by fussing about it…I don't want that sort. So when I die there'll be an end of me. I don't mind. I've done all I can for Oliver. He has lost the need for me. And the same sort of thing's to be gone through with Dolly…through she's no concern of yours…

EVAN: *(Thinking about it)* If you really think I can do something for the boy that no one else can.

MILDRED: You're so dry, Evan.

EVAN: Why should he thank us for tying this corpse of a story round his neck?

MILDRED: *(Business-like)* He doesn't get on with the Gauntletts. And he can hardly inherit. What with Victor's two sons… And it's a third on the way, I daresay. He was dutifully fond of Peckham, and Peckham liked him… Died when he was twelve though… So that's all they knew of each other. Peckham was no fool.

EVAN: I never thought so.

MILDRED: Except over women. But a sensible husband to me… It's my money Oliver gets. I saw to that. Are you going to marry Joan Westbury?

EVAN: I hope so.

MILDRED: You'd mind her knowing?

EVAN: Would you?

MILDRED: Oliver seems very fond of her.

EVAN: Does he?

MILDRED: When I saw you three in the garden together just now…

EVAN: Well?

MILDRED: I got ready to give him up. It's far likelier, when he's told, that he'll learn to hate me.

EVAN: And it's also possible, isn't it, that Joan might turn her back on the three of us.

MILDRED: I hadn't thought of that.

EVAN: I'm afraid I had.

MILDRED: Good God, Evan. And you'd let her?

EVAN: You credit me with the queerest powers.

MILDRED: If Joan finds she's jealous of me, let her take Oliver from me… That ought to satisfy her.

EVAN: I doubt if you understand Joan.

MILDRED: Well enough.

EVAN: And adopting him as my secretary or what not would prompt some people's memories…that was one good reason, I thought, for snubbing the boy. (*Looking down the gallery*) Here come the What's-his-names… American people…

MILDRED: Can they hear us?

EVAN: Not yet…. They're stopping to look at a picture.

(EVAN *and* MILDRED's *talk seems to be at an end. She adds a postcript.*)

MILDRED: I've wondered what the second housemaid felt like when she swore her baby on the footman.

EVAN: And the footman was adjured to have the feelings of a man. I'm sorry.

MILDRED: You'd better dress for dinner. I once gave you a dog. Did you get fond of it?

EVAN: Very. I'm afraid you can't shame me quite so easily.

MILDRED: Well, Oliver's going wrong…and it's breaking my heart.

EVAN: You'd cut bits out of yourself for him.

MILDRED: He is a bit cut out of me.

EVAN: Look out…

KITTREDGE: *(Off)* Is it my ignorance to suppose that a Hobbema?

MILDRED: *(To off)* We'll hope not, Mr Kittredge, as it is ear-marked for income tax.

(KITTREDGE and SUSAN appear; ready for dinner. He is an old man; she, a girl of grave simplicity.)

KITTREDGE: Very unfair, I agree, for any mere nobody to paint such a picture.

MILDRED: Evan, will you go and get dressed?

EVAN: Dear me…you're my hostess, aren't you?

MILDRED: I wait dinner twenty minutes and no more. British punctuality, Miss Susan.

EVAN: You count a hundred and walk to the hall and pick up the others, and you'll find me waiting by the soup tureen. And I'll trust to your honour for a measured hundred, Miss Kittredge… *(He hurries down the gallery and away.)*

MILDRED: Come along.

(MILDRED has to collect a half-dozen etceteras that women, dressed for dinner, carry round in a country house.)

KITTREDGE: This was your home, Lady Peckham?

MILDRED: Mamma started married life by being restless. I got born in Venice. But I grew here.

KITTREDGE: I know better than to be enthusiastic in England…so I won't remind you how beautiful it is.

MILDRED: You needn't. I know. Though it's ramshackle, all but the kitchens. They're Norman. You must see them. A bit of a nuisance to my brother now he can't keep it up. He could sell it to a Trade Union for a Convalescent Home. But we've a cousin who's gone into oil, and won't break the entail.

KITTREDGE: I picture a sick bricklayer meditating in the cloister upon his spiritual affinity to the men who built it…

MILDRED: I can picture him asleep over the Sunday paper. You're a professor, aren't you, Mr Kittredge?…

KITTREDGE: Emeritus.

MILDRED: And you are writing a book about us…

KITTREDGE: From sheer force of habit, I am collecting materials for a book I shall never write…

MILDRED: What's it called?

KITTREDGE: *The Selection of an Aristocracy* might serve for a title.

MILDRED: What does that mean?

KITTREDGE: The idea is not a new one, of course… That a community can only be kept self-respecting and powerful by courage in the continuing selection of an aristocracy.

MILDRED: Aren't they born?

SUSAN: One hundred.

MILDRED: What? Oh thank you.

(They begin to go.)

KITTREDGE: I ask your approval of Susan's upbringing. She does what she is told without comment.

MILDRED: Then she's both a very good girl and a very deceitful one.

KITTREDGE: She smiles. I always think that I know what she means when she smiles. But perhaps…

(They have disappeared.)

(End of Scene)

Scene 3

(Sunday, near lunch time. ELEANOR *alone with her letters and papers. Off on the terrace a very noisy game in progress.)*

DOLLY: *(Off)* 'Run, Joan! No, not a straighter…she'll get you. Stop at Apollo. Oh I knew she would! That's three games to them. Why didn't you stop at Apollo?

JOAN: *(Off)* But I have to do it in five, haven't I?

OLIVER: *(Off)* Well you'd do two to spare.

JOAN: *(Off)* No, I took three up.

OLIVER: *(Off)* Yes, she did…one to the Faun and one to Diana…

DOLLY: *(Off)* Susan, you're no end of a shot. Let's play women against men…and Evan may run twice.

EVAN: *(Off)* Miss Dorothy Gauntlett…do you know my age?

DOLLY: *(Off)* Fiddlededee! Look how Joan runs.

JOAN: *(Off)* Tactful child!

*(*ELEANOR *goes to the window and waves.)*

ELEANOR: Evan!

EVAN: *(Off)* What's that? I'll come up.

DOLLY: *(Off)* No, no, no! We can't play four.

ELEANOR: I won't keep him long.

DOLLY: *(Off)* Why do you desecrate the Sabbath by reading reports? Come down and play Straighters.

ELEANOR: I believe I last played Straighters, Dolly, the year before you were born.

DOLLY: *(Off)* Mother's a dab at it still.

(The game now stopped, the players seem to be resting beneath the window.)

SUSAN: *(Off)* Does that drawing in the library date its being invented?

DOLLY: *(Off)* It's older…because of the counting by chases. The tennis court was pulled down in seventeen-fifty…

(EVAN, a little the worse for his bout of straighters, comes in by the turret door, ELEANOR hands him a letter.)

OLIVER: *(Off)* It's only Rounders played straight up the Terrace.

ELEANOR: From Sir Curtis Henry.

EVAN: What's he plaguing you for?

ELEANOR: Duddington's been at him.

EVAN: He's been at me.

DOLLY: *(Off)* The paving makes your feet so hot…that's the worst.

ELEANOR: Why Sir Curtis should suppose that I could or would persuade you to stand as the Party nominee, I can't imagine.

SUSAN: *(Off)* Was this how Apollo and Diana got their arms broken?

EVAN: *(Finished the letter and gives it back)* Stockton-on-Couch is growing agitated evidently.

DOLLY: *(Off)* There used to be a rule in my young days not to touch the statues.

ELEANOR: But Duddington thinks you could carry it as an Independent, doesn't he?

EVAN: Duddington's job as an election agent is to find the greatest common measure of agreement...

DOLLY: *(Off)* Oliver, fetch us a towel.

OLIVER: *(Off)* What for?

EVAN: ...and to collar votes from the Anarchists, Christadelphians, Anti-vivisectionists, members of the Flat Earth Society...

DOLLY: *(Off)* We three females will go dabble our six hot feet in the fountain.

EVAN: *(Looks out the window)* Dolly, don't be a fool... you'll give yourselves frightful colds.

DOLLY: *(Off)* Silence, Methusaleh.

ELEANOR: Well, what shall I say to the valiantly tactful Sir Curtis?

DOLLY: *(Off)* Come along!

JOAN: *(Off)* No!

DOLLY: *(Off)* Joan Westbury...do you want me to carry you there like a sack of potatoes or a Sabine lady?

EVAN: Give him a taste of your quality. You'll be a candidate yourself yet.

JOAN: *(Off)* I shall ask your mother to put you on a lowering diet, Dolly.

EVAN: My part in the answer is that I'm still considering whether I'll stand at all.

DOLLY: *(Off)* I'd tuck Susan under my arm too for tuppence. Come along. Come along.

(And DOLLY can be heard whooping triumphantly along the terrace. The other two follow her, their voices tell us.)

SUSAN: *(Off)* Are you so hot?

JOAN: *(Off)* Only breathless…a little…

ELEANOR: Very well. I'll say that.

(EVAN starts to go, stops.)

EVAN: Have you read my notes on your report?

ELEANOR: I was just about to. You haven't told me what you make of it as a whole.

EVAN: It's dull.

ELEANOR: The Industrial Birth-rate is not a lively subject. Perhaps Part Two upon Wages of Young Persons will amuse you more.

EVAN: When is that to be ready?

ELEANOR: We still have the West Riding evidence to take.

EVAN: Shall I do a draft in rhyme for you?
Equal work for equal wages,
Boys and girls who read these pages.
Men and women through the ages.
Twelve disinterested sages
Have arrived by easy stages
At the…gages…cages…
But I fear my nonsense doesn't ring like Dolly's.

ELEANOR: Evan…since we passed the last of those proofs in September you haven't, as far as I know, done a stroke of work. You make a mock bow now and then to this Committee drudgery of mine…

EVAN: It must be. But you enjoy it.

ELEANOR: As long as I'm busy I'm happy, I fear.

EVAN: Don't be ashamed of that.

ELEANOR: Are we ever to begin our last volume?

(No response)

ELEANOR: I was looking at your discarded chapters only the other day.

EVAN: Any good?

ELEANOR: Very well written.

EVAN: Why is it, Eleanor, that for all your goodness and my cleverness, for all the assembled virtues of this jolly houseparty, and the good-will that's going begging throughout the world…how is it that we shan't establish the Kingdom of Heaven on earth by Tuesday week?

ELEANOR: We could be content with less.

EVAN: You were fully yourself at sixteen. You have been unwearied in well-doing. And I'm still a naughty boy. Have you never found that the whole world's turmoil is but a reflection of the anarchy in your own heart?

ELEANOR: No.

EVAN: That's where we differ, then.

ELEANOR: I fear you have always kept up appearances a little with me.

EVAN: I fear you have always believed in them.

ELEANOR: Well…if you're going into Bellingham's government…if you're going to marry Joan Westbury. When these trifles are settled, no doubt you'll tell me…

EVAN: Have you ever gone adventuring…dear good Eleanor…in your secret heart?

ELEANOR: I notice you call me good in the tone you might tell your wife…if you had one…that she was pretty….

(MILDRED, *as from church, comes in by the turret door, she is followed by* KITTREDGE.)

MILDRED: Morning, Evan.

EVAN: Been to church?

MILDRED: Sitting among the tombs of the Serocolds. I believe I wrecked my youthful eyesight reading those epitaphs in sermon time.

KITTREDGE: I was whisperingly commanded to translate the Latin ones.

MILDRED: I suspect your translations, Mr Kittredge.

KITTREDGE: There are more ways than one of reading most epitaphs.

MILDRED: I'd better write my own.

KITTREDGE: The work of a lifetime.

EVAN: Stephen go with you?

MILDRED: Haven't seen him. He ought to go to Church when he's here. It's not fair to the Rector. I like going. I much prefer saying my prayers in public…and it's the only place where they'll let me sing.

DOLLY: (*Off, from the gallery*) Evan…stand still…you're the winning post…stick your arms out.

(EVAN *does as he is bid.* KITTREDGE *moves a chair. We hear a skurrying.* DOLLY *and* JOAN *are racing neck and neck; the winning post reached,* JOAN *flings herself in a chair with "ay de mi!"* DOLLY *is barefoot.*)

DOLLY: Did I win?

EVAN: Not you.

DOLLY: Oh…I lose a pound…and I wanted one badly. You're nowhere.

(*This addressd to* SUSAN *who comes in a bad third*)

KITTREDGE: Susan if you mean to invest your small capital in racing you must do better.

DOLLY: No…she wasn't to pay if she lost…because she thinks betting's wrong.

SUSAN: I don't. I only said I didn't bet.

DOLLY: What about bare feet over the gravel for a handicap anyway?

SUSAN: I caught my dress on the big door.

ELEANOR: Joan.. ought you to run like that?

JOAN: But I won!

(ELEANOR *returns to her report, others settle;* DOLLY *in the window seat, oblivious to chills.*)

KITTREDGE: A granddaughter is a terrifying responsibility for an ignorant old man whose business it has been to theorise about life. But I think it a subtle form of cruelty to children to educate them in ideals that the world they will emerge into never means to abide by. So I try to fix Susan's attention upon the simple arithmetic of things. Is that wise?

MILDRED: Mr Kittredge you're a most accomplished flirt, and I only wish I were up to your form. Bait Eleanor for a bit…she's intellectual. I'll look on.

KITTREDGE: Miss Strowde is entrenched against frivolity.

ELEANOR: No.

(*A towel thrown through the window*)

DOLLY: Thank you, Oliver.

EVAN: Did you feel older at fifty, sir?

KITTREDGE: Much.

EVAN: That's cheering.

DOLLY: Mother…I've cut my great toe.

MILDRED: Wash it with Condy.

DOLLY: (*With some pride*) It's bleeding.

MILDRED: I don't believe I've ever felt any particular age. I sleep like a log…I don't dream…and every morning at half-past seven I wake up wide and say to myself: Hullo, here I am again.

KITTREDGE: What do you find fifty's worse symptom, Mr Strowde?

EVAN: That it's easy to stop and hard to begin.

KITTREDGE: Yes…if one stops to think…

DOLLY: Got a handkerchief, Oliver?

OLIVER: *(Off)* Dash it, I fetched you a towel. Wipe your nose on the corner.

DOLLY: I wish to blow my nose.

MILDRED: Really, Dolly!

DOLLY: Don't you want me to be clean?

MILDRED: Very, very clean, my darling…as you'll never be godly.

DOLLY: Thank God!

(STEPHEN comes down the gallery.)

STEPHEN: Good morning, guests.

MILDRED: Just up?

STEPHEN: Mildred…I was milking a cow on behalf of your breakfast at six-thirty.

EVAN: No one believes that, Stephen.

STEPHEN: It is very nearly true.

DOLLY: Uncle Stephen, will you lend me a pound?

STEPHEN: For how long is the accommodation required?

DOLLY: Till I can take you on at tennis.

STEPHEN: I do not play tennis for money.

DOLLY: But how mean of you when you've got some.

STEPHEN: *(To MILDRED)* No Bellingham for lunch.

MILDRED: Oh?

DOLLY: Well, he'd have been a bit tough… That is a joke.

STEPHEN: Telephones he has a toothache. Not even neuralgia.

MILDRED: Evan, who told him you were here?

EVAN: Stephen, I trust.

STEPHEN: He invited himself…he told me he wanted to meet you by accident.

EVAN: You are an incorrigible intriguer.

DOLLY: It's Oliver. The silly old snob won't lunch with a gaol-bird. Hurrah!

JOAN: Perhaps he has a toothache.

STEPHEN: You've not yet met our Prime Minister, Mr Kittredge?

KITTREDGE: Not for thirty years. I shall hope for another chance.

EVAN: Don't. Well…I'm unfair to the creature. I suppose. I retain a perverse affection for him. But the worst of democracy, don't you find, sir, is that it tends to breed these low forms of political life. You could slice bits off of Bellingham and each bit would wriggle off… And he'd find them all seats in Parliament…

DOLLY: Vote for Brooke Bellingham…our only bulwark against Bolshevisim.

STEPHEN: Dolly…I'll send you electioneering.

EVAN: Think of it. A line of alliteration between us and the abyss.

OLIVER: *(Off)* A bas Belinjam! Conspuez Brooke.

MILDRED: D'you think it's coming?

KITTREDGE: Why, we are living already, you may say,
under a dictation of the intellectual proletariat…and
how few of us complain. Yes, I think we must finally
be ruled by the people who provide us with what we
want most in the world. Comforts, power, or wisdom.
Artisan, king or philosopher. Which will you exalt?

EVAN: Not the philosopher, Mildred.

MILDRED: Think not? Why not?

EVAN: He'll always be finding fresh things for you to
do without. That makes his job easy for him.

MILDRED: *(Cheerily)* I wouldn't mind a revolution…if
Oliver and you and Stephen would run it.

STEPHEN: I will not. I'm tired.

MILDRED: But save us from cads.

KITTREDGE: Amen.

EVAN: Yes, when we consider what the gentlemen have
been capable of occasionally, God knows what the cads
may do.

MILDRED: Twenty years back, if we'd known it, was
our time for a good revolution.

DOLLY: It's never too late to smash.

MILDRED: I don't want any more killing.

DOLLY: *(Radiant in the sunshine by the window)* I tell you
though…women are going to fight in the next war.
And if we hurry up I can be in the Air Force. Susan, I'll
come and bomb your little head off, first thing.

SUSAN: Please do.

STEPHEN: How long do you stay in England, Mr
Kittredge?

KITTREDGE: Will you promise me a General Election by
November? Susan is studying politics, and she wants
to see one.

MILDRED: What on earth is she doing that for?

STEPHEN: I can't promise.

ELEANOR: I can provide you with more profitable study meanwhile.

SUSAN: Thank you, indeed. Lady Westbury says that she'll come back to Massachusetts with us, Grandfather.

JOAN: May I leave it at perhaps, for a little? But I've travelled Eastwards so much that it's time I went West, isn't it?

DOLLY: D'you mean die?

JOAN: I didn't.

STEPHEN: My dear Dolly.

DOLLY: That's what that means.

KITTREDGE: Please do come and see us, Lady Westbury, sitting in blankets before our wigwams.

JOAN: What must I bring to trade with?

KITTREDGE: Your heart.

SUSAN: Our woods are beautiful in the autumn.

JOAN: I thought you called it the Fall.

KITTREDGE: That sounds too sad, don't you think? But by November we're tucked up in snow very often.

JOAN: I may go on to Japan. Eva Currie wants me to... to be there by Christmas.

MILDRED: Dolly, go and make yourself half way decent for lunch.

DOLLY: *(Who knows an order when she hears one)* Yes, Mother.

EVAN: Die...how we hate the word. And we none of us really believe we're going to.

MILDRED: I believe it.

EVAN: Oh, we're ready to surrender what we've done with and don't value…

ELEANOR: The work of our minds lives on.

EVAN: By taking thought to? Show me a living faith, and I'll show it you careless of life. Dolly there, in her pride of body…

DOLLY: I say!

EVAN: …would jump out of that window for a sixpence.

DOLLY: I'll do it for a pound. Oliver's underneath.

EVAN: But this world of the mind we've made for ourselves is cumbered with things that we won't let die. Ask Oliver…if I yield to the temptation and go back to trying to help govern this ungrateful country, whether he'll promise to see me decently assassinated when I've done my devilmost?

DOLLY: (Head out the window) Oliver, will you please see Evan decently assassinated?

OLIVER: (Off) It hasn't been settled yet who's to be let off living…but he may choose his lamp-post on the chance.

EVAN: You'll be content, Mildred, if a little of you lives on in that child?

MILDRED: Heaven forbid I should worry her.

DOLLY: What a disgusting thought.

STEPHEN: Then don't you think it.

DOLLY: I won't. (She heads down the gallery.)

EVAN: Dolly, I'll toss you for a pound.

DOLLY: Oo! Suppose I lose.

EVAN: A month's credit.

DOLLY: Oo... (*She goes.*)

EVAN: The life of the mind is a prison in which we go melancholy mad. Better turn dangerous...and be done away with.

DOLLY: (*Off*) Evan.

EVAN: Hullo!

DOLLY: (*Off*) I'll risk it. Heads!

(EVAN *takes out a coin and tosses it.*)

KITTREDGE: There is, of course, that faculty we call the soul by which we may escape into uncharted regions.

EVAN: Heads it is!

DOLLY: (*Off*) Thank god...

KITTREDGE: But the rulers of men seldom seek them.

JOAN: Why?

KITTREDGE: A confusing place, the world where the soul wanders...made of mud and light...and mud sticks and light dazzles. Lonely...yet in it we can keep nothing of our own. For entering we abandon everything but hope...and hope is the lure.

JOAN: Towards what?

KITTREDGE: This is a secret.

JOAN: They can overhear.

KITTREDGE: ...Well known, and disbelieved. It's so discouraging. The soul of man is in the making still... we are experiments to be tried again and yet again... and the light lures us to extinction. Can you rule a country prosperously on such a creed? No...have a comfortable Kingdom of Heaven just round the corner...or who will take a step towards it?

EVAN: Besides, Stephen, you don't want this country governed.

STEPHEN: Truthfully, I think we want it kept amused at the moment…till we see what's going to happen next.

(The three men begin to head down the gallery; SUSAN *stands at the turret door;* ELEANOR *has finished the report and her brother's notes; she was been sitting very still.)*

EVAN: So I'm not your man.

ELEANOR: Evan.

EVAN: Yes.

ELEANOR: Are these notes for vulgar reading?

EVAN: My legacy to you.

KITTREDGE: I don't quite understand why Mr Bellingham hasn't dissolved before this.

STEPHEN: We can't get defeated in the House on any likely issue.

EVAN: Prisoned, minds, Mr Kittredge…and a world of power to be wielded that might stagger the purpose of Caesar. What the deuce will happen next? For all that I don't much care, I shake in my shoes.

(They are gone.)

MILDRED: What notes, Eleanor?

ELEANOR: Evan poking fun at my report.

*(SUSAN *goes out the turret door.)*

MILDRED: That's a strange, still girl. Is she stone cold inside, or just on the boil?

JOAN: I see great beauty in her.

MILDRED: Do you.

JOAN: It'll shine out in time.

MILDRED: I don't understand Americans. They're so solemn.

*(JOAN *heads down the gallery.)*

ELEANOR: They take things seriously.

MILDRED: And so devilish gay when they're gay.

ELEANOR: I don't find them hard to understand.

(*Silence,* ELEANOR *and* MILDRED *are alone.*)

MILDRED: We two old harridans, Eleanor!

ELEANOR: Thank you.

MILDRED: Between us, I expect, we've tasted most of the fat and the lean of life… Well…nothing tastes like it.

ELEANOR: You're worried about Oliver.

MILDRED: Not a bit.

ELEANOR: What took him to that meeting? Who encourages him in this foolishness?

MILDRED: I think he spins it out of his own inside.

ELEANOR: Well, as long as he behaves himself.

MILDRED: I hope he'll do more than that. I should get Evan married to Joan Westbury if I were you. That might settle him. Or are you too jealous of her?

ELEANOR: What an amazing question.

MILDRED: You're so consistent, Eleanor…that's what's the matter with you.

ELEANOR: There's little I could do…in any case.

MILDRED: Were you ever in love?

ELEANOR: Once.

MILDRED: What happened?

ELEANOR: Nothing.

MILDRED: If you hate Joan, try putting a little poison in her soup…. And then getting on your knees to ask God to forgive you for it.

(ELEANOR *and* MILDRED *have collected their belongings,
and move now for lunch.*)

ELEANOR: A little hard on her…

(ELEANOR *and* MILDRED *head down the gallery.*)

(*End of Scene*)

Scene Four

(*It is Sunday evening about ten o'clock.* JOAN *sits alone by
the open window; she has turned out the light near her, but
those farther down the gallery are apparent. After a moment*
OLIVER's *voice from below:*)

OLIVER: (*Off*) Lady Westbury.

JOAN: Yes.

OLIVER: (*Off*) May I come up?

JOAN: You may. (*When she realizes that he is climbing up:*)
Oliver! You'll kill yourself!

(OLIVER's *head and shoulders appear in the window. he
stops, a little breathless. This is something of a feat for a one-
armed man.*)

OLIVER: That wasn't so bad. Now comes the pull…
If you take hold we'll both tumble. Hold your breath
and think hard. Now! (*With great effort he flings himself
over the window-sill into the room, and rolls on the floor. He
picks himself up.*) And I'm not drunk, am I?

JOAN: You shouldn't run such risks.

OLIVER: I was last night…on one half glass of claret.
Nobody noticed. Tonight I've had a bottle of port to
my own whack…and I'm so sober that it hurts. May I
sit and talk to you?

JOAN: Yes.

OLIVER: Shall I try not to talk about myself?

JOAN: No, I'd like you to.

(*A short pause*)

OLIVER: Why won't Evan take me on?

JOAN: He hasn't told me.

OLIVER: They say you're going to marry him.

JOAN: Do they? Well...shall I?

OLIVER: Don't ask me. What am I to do, please, if Evan won't take me on?

JOAN: Is he your only hope?

OLIVER: He's in my way.

JOAN: What does that mean?

OLIVER: Sounds like a plot to blow him sky high one day as he walks into Downing Street. I think I did make Uncle Stephen believe at dinner that I'd been sworn into at least one secret society...for all he pretended not to.

JOAN: It's Mr Serocold's business, I suppose, to take such things seriously.

OLIVER: Yes it is. So why doesn't he? Tell them the truth and they don't believe you.

JOAN: I will.

OLIVER: The men with the secrets that count will know each other when the times comes, won't they?

JOAN: That sounds dangerous. Why is Evan in your way?

OLIVER: I wonder what it is in one that picks out a man or a woman. Evan was picked out for me, you may say. Mother has always been fond of him. My father was fond of him. I remember saying once, when I was eight, that I meant to grow to be like him.

JOAN: And you're not fond of many people.

OLIVER: I hate most people…when I come to think of it.

JOAN: Is that why it hurts you to be sober? But tell me how one soberly hates people. I don't think I know.

OLIVER: Well, you can't love the mob, surely. Because that's to be one of them…chattering, and scolding and sniveling and cheering…maudlin drunk, if you like. I learned to be soldier enough to hate a mob.

JOAN: How long have you been so unhappy?

OLIVER: Don't think I'm out after happiness, please.

JOAN: Do you ever pray, Oliver?

OLIVER: All the time. Whenever I'd a hard job on in the City I'd walk there in the morning praying like fun. If I hadn't prayed my way in at this window I'd have broken my neck. I pray all the time.

JOAN: How old are you? I forget.

OLIVER: I believe I'm still eighteen.

JOAN: How's that?

OLIVER: Years don't count for much, do they…as against memory, say? Parts of me seem to forget all about the war…but there's some part of me doesn't. I've an idea I don't grow any older now…and when I come to die it'll seem an odd out-of-date sort of catastrophe. I'm furious that I'm still alive at all. I used to pray night after night at school that I'd be killed when I got to France.

JOAN: That was perverse of you…to be fighting against our prayers.

OLIVER: Oh, once I was there I didn't mind saving my skin. But I tell you…this is a beast of a world to have left on one's hands.

(A little silence)

JOAN: Well, what are you going to do about it?

OLIVER: Destroy.

JOAN: What?

OLIVER: All I can learn to.

JOAN: Didn't you see enough destruction?

OLIVER: A futile sort. My firm bought a lot of shares
and we thought we had a mine in Eastern Galicia…
so I was sent out two years ago to see. The town was
a rubbish heap. Typhus had done well too. But there
they were breeding children to build it all up again….
That being the cheapest way. So if we can't do some
better destroying than that who'll ever be able to make
a fresh start? Save me from weary people with their No
More War. What we want is a real one.

JOAN: And where's the enemy?

OLIVER: If I knew where I shouldn't be sitting here
helpless. I'm looking for him. But we're tricked so
easily… This world's all tricks, isn't it?

JOAN: And what has Evan to teach you?

OLIVER: I want to find out how it is he has failed.

JOAN: Has he failed, then?

OLIVER: Yes…and you'll have to comfort him for it if
you marry him.

JOAN: But wise men like your uncle say that if he'll take
office again, now the bunglers have had a chance…
there's his career still. And he wasn't a failure in office
before.

OLIVER: He'll need more comfort than that, if I'm right
about him. Nothing's much easier, is it, than to make
that sort of success if you've the appetite for it. Find a
few ready-made notions to exploit. But Evan set out to
get, past all tricks, to the heart of things…didn't he?

JOAN: The very tallest of us ask for comfort sometimes.

OLIVER: Evan won't take me on because he's afraid of me.

JOAN: Nonsense.

OLIVER: I can tell he's afraid of me. Why? Because he knows that I know he has failed. And he knows that I hate him for it.

JOAN: Very wicked nonsense, Oliver!

OLIVER: Oh, do him in with comfort if you like. Trick him. Do your best, dear Evan, and no man can do more in this worst-of-all possible worlds. If he had any self-respect left in him he'd thank you to hate him rather.

JOAN: You're very like him.

OLIVER: Am I?

JOAN: Oh...not in any ordinary sense. Am I to ask Evan to take you on?

OLIVER: Yes...

JOAN: If you came to understand him you might learn not to hate him...

OLIVER: Yes, there's that danger.

JOAN: Oliver, you never laugh now, I've noticed.

OLIVER: At myself?

JOAN: Well, that's a simple form of destruction. You might try it to begin with.

(OLIVER *stands; stung, as she meant he should be.*)

OLIVER: Good night.

JOAN: I've made you angry.

OLIVER: No. I was off on my walk when I saw you at the window.

JOAN: Every night...wet or fine...how many miles?

OLIVER: Seven or eight...till I'm too tired to think.

JOAN: The night is all one's own, isn't it…if only the inconsiderate sun wouldn't rise.

OLIVER: Is that how you comfort me? There's no need, thank you. I've not failed yet. Good night, Joan.

JOAN: But mind your prayers, Oliver.

(OLIVER *goes to the door.*)

JOAN: Not by the window again?

OLIVER: Too easy.

JOAN: Goodnight, then, my dear.

(OLIVER *goes.*)

(*End of Scene*)

Scene Five

(*It is Monday morning, a little after nine.* SIR LESLIE HERIOT, *in motoring things, comes striding along as if looking for some one. He glances out the window; then faces down the gallery again just as* EVAN's *voice is heard from the other end.*)

EVAN: (*Off*) Hullo, Heriot.

HERIOT: Hullo, Strowde…

EVAN: (*Off*) What are you doing here?

HERIOT: Came to run Stephen up to town. Good morning, Miss Strowde.

ELEANOR: (*Off*) Good morning, Sir Leslie.

(EVAN *appears,* ELEANOR *must be lagging behind.*)

EVAN: You must have left early.

HERIOT: Seven o'clock. I've not been at home…week-ending at Eckersley…it's sixty miles…the road must be better through Basingstoke. How are you?

EVAN: I'm alive.

HERIOT: Get any talk with Bellingham yesterday?

EVAN: He didn't come.

HERIOT: I knew he wouldn't.

EVAN: How's your job nowadays?

HERIOT: There's enough to do without making more. But I'm up to the trick of it this time. Let your office fellows pull the cart while you drive.

EVAN: That is undoubtedly the whole art of government.

HERIOT: And take time to think. I used to keep my nose buried in papers eight hours a day. Now I send for the men who write them…and size them up instead. *(To off)* How is my Women's Industry committee getting on, Miss Strowde?

(ELEANOR appears.)

ELEANOR: We're making the interim report you asked for.

HERIOT: *(With entire honesty)* Did I? Does this fellow help you out at all?

(ELEANOR who—how surprising—has not come to talk to HERIOT, is searching the writing table.)

ELEANOR: Surely I did leave my spectacles…

EVAN: *(Answering)* Not at all.

HERIOT: And the great history's finished?

ELEANOR: No.

HERIOT: I hear you're coming out into politics.

ELEANOR: I think not.

HERIOT: But do…it's great fun. No, perhaps you're right. We need intellectual spade-work…

EVAN: *(found the spectacles)* Here they are.

ELEANOR: Thank you. *(She goes.)*

HERIOT: Strowde…have we got to fight you at the election?

EVAN: Who said I was going to stand?

HERIOT: But you are.

EVAN: I've been asked to.

HERIOT: I know all about it.

EVAN: When is it to be…secrets apart?

HERIOT: I doubt if the old man has started to make up his mind. November…February.

EVAN: You think you'll come back?

HERIOT: Who else can? Look here…is it only Bellingham stands in the way?

EVAN: Of…?

HERIOT: …your coming back to us?

EVAN: Oh, dear, no.

HERIOT: What else?

EVAN: Why do you want me?

HERIOT: My dear fellow…am I to flatter you?

EVAN If you think it advisable.

HERIOT: Well, I won't. I'll come straight to the point. I came here this morning to come to the point with you.

EVAN: Good.

HERIOT: It's two years since I told Bellingham how vital I felt it to be for the Party to get you back. I've given him till now to make it up with you. Well, now I'm ready to say that sine qua non…sine qua non me! We must find you a seat again, and a seat in the Cabinet, after the election.

EVAN: I've found the seat, Heriot.

HERIOT: Even if we fight you there?

EVAN: Do your damnedest.

HERIOT: I don't want to.

EVAN: Bellingham's getting a bit feeble, is he?

HERIOT: D'you hear people say that?

EVAN: If he'll take me at your dictation it'll show the Gang, won't it, that you've got a strangle hold on him? And it'll show you that he feels you've got the Party behind you.

HERIOT: That's very tortuous.

EVAN: Tortuous…but not very tortuous. How soon do you think you'll be strong enough to kick him out?

HERIOT: Strowde…I cannot humour your brutality. I am a realist, I hope….

EVAN: As a detached observer, I've been giving you a couple of years.

HERIOT: If you think this intellectual ruthlessness of yours is a strength, you're wrong…it's a weakness. People don't answer to it…and political facts most certainly never answer to it.

EVAN: What the devil, my dear Heriot is a political fact?

HERIOT: As an undersecretary the old man declares he never knew what you'd say next. No wonder he thinks that in the Cabinet you'll be the death of him.

EVAN: I daresay I should be.

HERIOT: But I tell him we must consider your essential value. You certainly will find him feebler. But after a year or two of the old hard grind I'm pretty confident you'd find yourself…subdued to what you work in.

EVAN: And with?

HERIOT: Or with. The potter's hand. Statesmanship…so I phrase it…is the art of dealing with men as they most illogically are, and with the time as it nearly always most unfortunately is. We hope for the better…we strive for the better. Never let us cease to proclaim that. But the day's work must be done.

EVAN: You're making a fool of yourself over the Trusts.

HERIOT: D'you think so? Why do you think so?

EVAN: Your figures are wrong.

HERIOT: They're official figures. Salomons said something of the sort to me six months ago. But we are faced with the demand for a bill.

EVAN: It being the business of the legislature to legislate.

HERIOT: God knows I'd be glad to drop it. Where were we?

EVAN: Do you mind my sister joining the discussion?

HERIOT: Not at all. I never make mysteries.

EVAN: *(Lifting his voice)* Eleanor…spare us a minute.

HERIOT: And I'm sure Miss Strowde is the soul of discretion.

(ELEANOR *appears again.*)

ELEANOR: Yes.

EVAN: We two have worked in unison for so long.

HERIOT: Well…to write history or to make it…that is the question.

ELEANOR: The writing should warn one to be rather more particular in the making, Sir Leslie.

EVAN: The practical question is…could Heriot and I between us get rid of Bellingham the sooner? I might

put that problem to the old gentleman if he sends for
me.

HERIOT: Thank you.

EVAN: Adding, of course, that you scouted the very
idea when I so much as hinted it…Bellingham's sixty-
seven. He has poor health. He has been twice Prime
Minister. He ought to be able to measure by now the
amount of annoyance he can endure. And you don't
suppose that when you were putting your sine qua
non this idea didn't occur to him.

HERIOT: I can't help his suspicious nature.

EVAN: Of course we must think of our country.

HERIOT: Your humour eludes me.

EVAN: Then there's a further possible question…how
long would it take me after to get rid of you?

HERIOT: Let's be serious. Serocold's waiting for me.

EVAN: You repeat your offer?

HERIOT: What's your alternative? Look at this present
opposition…sitting like a row of turnips…

EVAN: Or shall I stick to intellectual spade-work?

HERIOT: You're restless. You'll get back to the House
and you won't have enough to do there. You'll grow
depressed and dyspeptic and you'll take to making
acid interruptions inaudible in the press gallery.
You'll find yourself chief of a little group of righteous
high-brows in passionate agreement upon abstract
principles, without an interest in common and
considering themselves insulted if you ask them to
vote solid.

EVAN: Now here is a wise man, Eleanor…a
disillusioned man.

(HERIOT's *glance goes by chance down the gallery.*)

HERIOT: Who's this?

EVAN: Lady Westbury.

HERIOT: Do I know her?

EVAN: You must have known Mark Westbury.

HERIOT: Oh yes…useful fellow…Egypt did for him.

(So much for Mark.)

EVAN: The prospect of a fight over the inheritance would amuse Bellingham. He wouldn't think the worse of you…and he'd like me the better for it.

HERIOT: So he would…

(JOAN appears.)

JOAN: Good morning.

HERIOT: How d'you do, Lady Westbury? I fear you don't remember me…Leslie Heriot.

JOAN: Yes, indeed. You once gave me tea in your big room in Whitehall after my husband had been waiting for you three hours and a half.

HERIOT: Strong Indian tea…and you hated it.

JOAN: Not the tea, I'm sure.

HERIOT: The cake then…office cake.

JOAN: Perhaps it was the cake.

HERIOT: When are you coming to town, Strowde?

EVAN: Wednesday morning.

HERIOT: Lunch with me. Good-bye, Miss Strowde. Don't think me a cynic. I respect ideals. But I test them…as life tests them.

EVAN: My sister really thinks of us both as being about ten years old. I've been a trouble to her, Heriot…and her fear is now that I may corrupt your happy faith in life.

HERIOT: Try.

ELEANOR: Nothing would, Sir Leslie, I'm sure.

STEPHEN: (*Off*) Heriot, are you ready?

HERIOT: Coming.

STEPHEN: (*Off*) I must be at the office by eleven.

EVAN: But if we're to be fellow-conspirators, we must agree on a creed? We'll open Cabinet meetings by having this repeated, all standing...I believe that men cease to be fools to become knaves, and that we must govern them by fear and with lies. They will work under threat of starvation. Greed makes them cunning.

STEPHEN: (*Off*) Evan...I shall be late back.

EVAN: Wait a minute...but desire makes them dangerous. If they rightly remembered yesterday, they wouldn't get out of their beds tomorrow. Sleep's the great ally of the rulers of this world...for it rounds each day with oblivion.

HERIOT: That's a creed I should keep to myself. Goodbye, Lady Westbury.

JOAN: Good-bye.

(HERIOT *now takes* EVAN's *arm and starts down the gallery as a ship might leave a bay, with such swelling sails.*)

HERIOT: I am a democrat.... With certain reservations... The freer democracy the firmer must be the guiding hand. Do not expect to find in the masses a grasp of the principles upon which we base our actions. Appeal rather to the heart of the people...

(EVAN *and* HERIOT *disappear.* ELEANOR *and* JOAN *wait for a decent thirty seconds.*)

JOAN: I remember Mark saying after that interview... Deliver us from clean-shaven young Ministers, with busts of Napoleon on the mantelpiece.

ELEANOR: He caricatures himself now. Evan shouldn't poke fun of him so recklessly.

JOAN: By the time the sting penetrates he's thinking of something else.

EVAN: *(Returning)* One can't help liking him.

ELEANOR: I can. What is his offer worth?

EVAN: It was worth while manoeuvring him into making it. The next move is Bellingham's. No hurry for mine.

ELEANOR: Thank you for letting me hear you talk, Evan. I see I can be no more use to you. You're my brother...I thought I knew you...you've become a stranger to me. I fear there's only one thing I believe in...choosing a cause to serve it single-mindedly. I worked at your book with you. What does it mean to me to feel that if I burned every copy now, you'd hardly shrug your shoulders...and to find this task of mine...this report spattered with your mockeries. I sat up last night crying over it like a child over a copy-book. From today, please, let's pretend to be like-minded no more. Turn in your tacks and be the thing you despise. Does it matter? The curse is on you, it seems, of coming at last to despise whatever you do and are. I'm sorry...but I must save myself...from despair.

(Silence)

EVAN: That's clearly put...and quite indisputable.

ELEANOR: Perhaps I shouldn't have said so much before you, Joan. Perhaps I've been right to.

EVAN: I shall now have to advertise... Wanted, a political hostess...

(In silence, ELEANOR, unhurriedly, but with neither another word nor a look, gets up and goes out by the turret door.)

EVAN: Or will you save me a sovereign's worth of Agony column, Joan, and take the job?

JOAN: No, I can't.

(EVAN *looks at* JOAN; *then refuses the words' meaning.*)

EVAN: Am I to tell Bellingham and his gang, then to go to the devil without me? By all means.

JOAN: That's another matter.

EVAN: Do you mean you won't marry me, Joan?

JOAN: I can't.

(*Now* EVAN *must take the meaning, and he does.*)

EVAN: How long since you made up your mind to say this? You could have given me some sign. I've been taking things too much for granted.

JOAN: I did, too.

EVAN: What has happened? What have I done? What has changed you?

JOAN: I love you still.

EVAN: Don't say that.

JOAN: But…let me be.

EVAN: So I did! …But let's say no more for the moment. I see what's wrong. We mustn't try to live out the fag-end of a difficult past. We must start fresh.

JOAN: When the war was at its worst, they say you were at your hopefullest. I see why they want you to work with… You'll lose little in losing the last of me.

EVAN: I want you.

JOAN: How did you find your way into the dream that my true life is? I wish you never had. The selfish soul of me might have died the sooner, left lonely…and who'd have been the wiser then? I could have done

my duty to the end...married again, even...headed a
dinner table...not yours, though.

EVAN: Why not mine as well as another?

JOAN: Should I have liked you if I'd never loved you, I
wonder?

EVAN: The answer is that you did, you know.

JOAN: And we couldn't let well alone. But you're free
of me now. I set you free. Oh, this has been a jealous
devil, like all barren things.

EVAN: Barren?

JOAN: Ask your heart...and your own life ever since.
God forgive us... It isn't that one sits idle. I've known
how to be kind...I've hated evil...when I've suffered
loss I've suffered indeed. But none of it has truly
mattered. My boys...yes, a bad blow. And when
Eleanor came tip-toeing with the news from Cairo I let
grief have its will of me...I knew I so safely could...and
I slipped the more easily out of its clutches back into
my dream. And we agreed to be glad, you remember,
that I could still care for Mark.

EVAN: I said I understood that. I fear I lied to you. I
never did.

JOAN: He was very good to me. So would you be. One
must live honourably. But all the while I was half
ashamed to be giving him what I valued so little. And
you want what's left.

EVAN: This is merely morbid, Joan.

JOAN: Is it? I've laughed at myself. I've prayed...these
past weeks with your eyes on me...for some miracle
to give birth in me to anything wholly human that I
could bring you. I do think that if I could once go quite
obliviously to sleep I might wake up different.

EVAN: I didn't know you weren't sleeping well again.

JOAN: Evan, has one to die to sleep? Well surely then there'll be an end to this terrible constant consciousness…of purposeless being.

EVAN: You're not in your doctor's sense, ailing, are you, except for this? You've seemed so well and gay.

JOAN: He can't make me sleep…and he can't keep me still. I'm one of Nature's pranks, I tell him…quite conscienceless now, quite irresponsible.

EVAN: You'd better marry me then, Joan. I'll find you lots to do…work you to death by midnight. You shall sleep like a log and wake every morning a different woman. I'll be a perfectly selfish husband, I promise you. Think how a bride will deck my election platform. And you must flatter me, please, with constant affection… Would it help to find things to forgive me?

JOAN: *(With a half-smile)* Oh I've tried that…I'd so like to make you happy. Give me your hand.

EVAN: Give me yours.

(With an amused smile JOAN *lifts it and looks at it rather disparagingly.)*

JOAN: This?

EVAN: Marry me.

JOAN: Some other time. Go to work and forget me. *(Pause)* I'm done.

END OF ACT TWO

ACT THREE

Scene One

(EVAN's house in Bedford Square. A big writing table between windows. Another smaller table)

(It is a morning in March, and foggy without. EVAN is at his desk, OLIVER comes in, carrying a time-table and some opened letters. He does not speak, and has time to go to the smaller table to put them down, as well as to glance at a few others left there for him, before EVAN says, habitually, and hardly looking up from his own writing:)

EVAN: Morning.

OLIVER: Morning, sir.

EVAN: I thought you'd be late in this fog.

OLIVER: I walked. Will you make up the diary now?

EVAN: Yes.

(OLIVER deals with diary and letters and timetable with a Chief-of-Staff air.)

OLIVER: Unless you motor half the night I don't see that you can speak for Hughes at Neath on the twenty-first and at Dover the next afternoon.

EVAN: Cut Dover. Philpot will lose the seat anyhow.

OLIVER: I'm keeping four free days for emergencies in that fortnight.

EVAN: Get me *The Bible*, will you? I want to verify…I think it's First Kings, nineteen. I must go to Nottingham. There's a letter…

OLIVER: Yes…for the Saturday. And a solid four at Stockton, Tuesday to polling day…will that be right?

EVAN: Ask Duddington.

OLIVER: He has rung up to say he may take the twelve-forty down today and not wait for us. *(With the Bible now; he sets a press cutting on the table.)* Did you see this?

EVAN: *(Quick glance) The Guardian*?

OLIVER: They're all ducking and dodging over the Trust question.

EVAN: Naturally.

OLIVER: *(With The Bible)* What's the quotation?

EVAN: "Now, O Lord take away my life, for I am not better than my fathers." Very modern and progressive and disillusioned of Elijah. Why ever should he expect to be?

OLIVER: Verse four.

EVAN: Thank you.

OLIVER: And these to go back in the History file?

('These' are some manuscripts piled on the table.)

EVAN: Please.

OLIVER: Clumbermere's coming at three, you know.

EVAN: Yes. Did you see my sister? Has she gone out?

OLIVER: She said she was expecting Miss Kittredge to call for her at eleven.

EVAN: *(Back to the election)* I doubt if it'll be such a walk over.

OLIVER: For you…at Stockton.

EVAN: The whole election.

OLIVER: Well…you like a good fight.

EVAN: *(Genially)* You want us whacked. Traitor.

OLIVER: Not more than enough to hurt.

EVAN: If we were, Bellingham'd throw up the leadership.

OLIVER: Then a year or two's opposition would pay you.

EVAN: Personally…yes…with anything worth opposing. How much longer do you mean to stay with me, Oliver?

OLIVER: That's still for you to say.

EVAN: You must see that the sweets of office life don't quite spoil your old appetite for revolution. Put this straight…it's the speech for Thursday…and type that bit of it in triplicate.

OLIVER: *(With the manuscripts)* Why do you get all this stuff out night after night?

EVAN: My derelict past. I've been looking for what I could steal from it. Live stuff…almost. You've read it?

OLIVER: You said I might.

EVAN: I wanted you to.

OLIVER: Who else ever has?

EVAN: No one. Eleanor typed those three chapters you're holding. The rest…no one.

OLIVER: Why did none of it find a way into the four upstanding volumes?

EVAN: First it was to be for the first, you know…and then for the last.

OLIVER: And now there's to be no last.

EVAN: Do you feel like writing one?

OLIVER: Whenever a thought was precious to you…you hid it away here.

EVAN: Whenever it was not current coin…I laid it by. A queer task…bestowing the love of one's mind… Scraps of me, too unsure of utterance. As if this flimsiness itself could cohere and live. Well, I bequeath it to you, Oliver…this much of the failure you were so keen to track down. Burn it. It's just worth destroying.

OLIVER: But better inherit a failure, I suppose…for there's something to be done with it…than a success.

EVAN: That sounds quite wise. Are you growing patient?

OLIVER: I'm turning coward perhaps.

EVAN: I doubt it. What has happened?

OLIVER: I'm lonely.

EVAN: Why, of course.

OLIVER: I meant to live with the dead. I felt I must never forget them. But they're dead to me now. I used to find courage by mustering in the dark that regiment of fellows…I've marched miles with them night after night. One crack regiment, I thought, temptation proof, could make an end of the muddle you've made. And you'd be glad enough when the time came. But the time never comes, you told me. Damnable of you.

EVAN: I'm sorry.

OLIVER: (*Laughs*) Never mind. I'm busy. I'm growing hopeful and helpless and almost good natured. Don't give me away, though.

EVAN: Have we begun to impress even you…the gang of us…with our statesmen-like airs? Do you thrill at the sight of the red-leather dispatch-box with First Lord of the Treasury on it and an Urgent slip sticking out? You must take a cold chisel to the lock of it the first time it comes to me.

OLIVER: But I can't see what's to stop you, Evan, from being thrust to the top of this muddle of minds.

EVAN: No…quite immodestly…nor can I.

OLIVER: I watch them sizing you up. They don't like you.

EVAN: Why should they?

OLIVER: Why do they trust you, then?

EVAN: I'm not altogether one of them…and they've lost the habit of trusting each other.

OLIVER: Heriot thought he was making a smart move when he had you handed the hardest job going. This Clumbermere business.

EVAN: Do you think he wants me to fail at it?

OLIVER: No. I think he hopes that some sorry moment will give him a chance to wring your hand and say: well, never mind, old man.

EVAN: Yes, I can hear him.

OLIVER: Mulready wants to quarrel with you.

EVAN: I can't oblige Mulready.

OLIVER: What, not with one little row, and then kiss and be friends…instead of flattering him till he feels a perfect fool?

EVAN: He is…and if he wasn't kept in mind of it he'd become a nuisance.

OLIVER: You do treat Uncle Stephen as a fellow creature.

EVAN: One's fond of Stephen.

OLIVER: But I sit and watch you thresh out a scheme with some man…who's honest and capable at least. How is it he doesn't see that you're mocking him?

EVAN: No…I assure you.

OLIVER: Every letter I write for you…it's like laying a snare.

EVAN: Why…am I not theirs very faithfully, their most obedient humble servant? If the schemes will come to nothing in the end, is the mockery mine? What do you expect of me, Oliver?

OLIVER: Poor devils. Each one of them believes in something. If it's not in what he's doing it's in what he hopes to be…even if it's only in what he has failed to be. I suppose he expects you to believe a little in him.

EVAN: That's unreasonable. Are you still out to destroy? I'm showing you the sure way. It's to fulfill. The reddest revolutionary is but a part of what he turns against. It's the destiny of a spiritual generation to destroy itself by fulfilling its faith and completing its work…and we dignify our passions to this end. Not so pleasant, I grant you, to be doing one's share of the job cold-heartedly and open-eyed. But disbelief's a power…and power is satisfying. I lived half my life in the happiness…and unhappiness of a vision. One fine day I find that the world I'm living in is nothing like the idea of the world I've been living by. It comes quite casually…conversion to disbelief. But you know it's the truth you've found by finding you've always known it…known all along that your vision was a vision and no more.

OLIVER: And you leave happiness and unhappiness behind?

EVAN: You cease to suffer…you cease to hope. You have no will to be other than you are. You are, therefore, extraordinarily efficient. Be something ruthlessly...what else counts? And let life become what it will. Watch me succeed, Oliver. That will teach you how to down me in turn. It's the best service I can do you.

OLIVER: Wouldn't you sooner I killed you now where you sit?

EVAN: That would be rash and well-meaning of you... and hardly worth while.

OLIVER: When I was small you were jolly to me...and I liked that. Three times, I think Mother has started to try and tell me about...us three. I've managed to stop her...for where was the need...which, in every sense that counts, I believe I've always known.

(EVAN *has nothing to say, but...*)

EVAN: Have you? (*He looks at* OLIVER.)

OLIVER: Don't. We can't begin to be fond of each other.

EVAN: I hope nothing I ever said seemed to give your mother away.

OLIVER: Oh no. There was one fellow at school...he had some damned story about her inside him, I could see. So I made row with him...though scrapping wasn't the thing...and as near killed him as was decent.

(*Door opens,* STEPHEN.)

STEPHEN: Sorry, I'm late.

EVAN: You'll be later at Number Ten.

STEPHEN: The PM always keeps me waiting. Slack's the word.

EVAN: Here's what I'm going to say on Thursday. Oliver'll type you a copy.

(STEPHEN *takes the few sheets of paper.*)

STEPHEN: You seeing Clumbermere?

EVAN: Three o'clock.

STEPHEN: His people won't like this, will they?

EVAN: They're not meant to.

STEPHEN: I'm very sure Bellingham won't.

EVAN: He need not, either.

STEPHEN: But, my dear fellow, this is a pledge.

EVAN: Well…I'm nobody. I'm not in the government….
I'm not even in the House yet. If I choose to stake my
small reputation that the Trust question will have to be
squared inside those lines, what does it matter?

(STEPHEN hands him back the damned thing:)

STEPHEN: How long will it take you, Oliver?

OLIVER: Three minutes. *(He goes off with it.)*

STEPHEN: Evan…you are difficult.

EVAN: I've gruelled at this business, my dear Stephen,
till I know its necessities…and we'll have to come to
their heel.

STEPHEN: In time.

EVAN: And I know Clumbermere. He has got his
Bellinghams and Heriots and Stephen Serocolds to deal
with too. So I give him a pistol, you see, to put at their
heads, and he gives me one to put at yours.

STEPHEN: But surely if we must offend our own
people we might at least get some support out of
Clumbermere's lot for doing so.

EVAN: Good Lord…we don't want their support. Then
Clumbermere would have to start bargaining with us
for a great deal more than it's good to give him. He
knows that too.

STEPHEN: But I've to persuade Number Ten.

EVAN: Tell Number Ten that if I'm right it's all right…
and if I'm wrong they'll be rid of me.

(Door opens and ELEANOR *looks in.)*

ELEANOR: Evan, are you busy?

EVAN: Yes… Come in.

ELEANOR: *(To behind her)* Come in, my dear.

(This is SUSAN KITTREDGE, *who then follows her.* ELEANOR
shakes hands silently with STEPHEN*)*

EVAN: Good morning, Miss Susan.

ELEANOR: Bad news. Joan's very ill.

STEPHEN: Joan Westbury?

SUSAN: A letter from my grandfather this morning.

STEPHEN: Is she still out there?

SUSAN: Since Christmas.

ELEANOR: May Evan read it?

SUSAN: Of course.

*(*SUSAN *has it in her hand.* EVAN *takes it without a word.)*

STEPHEN: What's the matter with her?

ELEANOR: *(Touching her head)* Tumour…

SUSAN: Grandfather didn't know for a while that she
wasn't sleeping at all. Now she'd had a doctor from
Boston that he says he can trust.

(To EVAN *who is silently intent on the letter:)*

SUSAN: I'm afraid it's dreadfully illegible…he never
types.

STEPHEN: Are they operating?

ELEANOR: They won't. They give her a few weeks.

STEPHEN: When was that written?

ELEANOR: Ten days ago.

STEPHEN: I suppose they dose her with morphia.

ELEANOR: Surely.

STEPHEN: I must go.

(After all, what can be done, and what more can be said? Glancing at EVAN, *he goes out.* ELEANOR *and* SUSAN *talk in lowered voices:)*

ELEANOR: What a worry for your grandfather. He's being most kind. You've been crying.

SUSAN: I do the usual things I'm afraid.

ELEANOR: Never be afraid of doing the usual things.

*(*EVAN *suddenly speaks, and* ELEANOR *and* SUSAN *both turn.)*

EVAN: This is from Countesbury? Massachusetts?

SUSAN: Yes.

*(*EVAN *goes back to reading.)*

ELEANOR: I thought she was ill in the summer. Why... she had planned to go on to Japan, hadn't she, Evan?

*(*STEPHEN *looks in again with the paper that* OLIVER *has typed. He says softly:)*

STEPHEN: Goodbye, Eleanor. Let me know when you hear again, please.

ELEANOR: You're dining tomorrow.

STEPHEN: Oh...yes. *(To* SUSAN*)* Goodbye...

SUSAN: Goodbye.

*(*STEPHEN *disappears.* EVAN's *intent stillness—for the letter is long and not easily read—sets up a strain. It is half to relieve it that* SUSAN *says:)*

SUSAN: I'll write today...but it'll miss the mail. I'm sure grandfather would have cabled if she were...worse.

ELEANOR: She's dying, my dear.

SUSAN: I know…though I don't understand really.

ELEANOR: That is as it should be. If we thought often of dying we should soon think of nothing else. Time enough, then, for you.

SUSAN: But…

(EVAN *has finished the letter, has risen, and with a curt 'Thank you' he hands it back and goes out.*)

ELEANOR: Twenty past ten, is it?

SUSAN: Just.

ELEANOR: When did you last hear from Joan herself?

SUSAN: Two weeks ago.

ELEANOR: Was she ill then, when she wrote…did she say?

SUSAN: No. But that may have been because…we were playing a childish game…I did once start to tell you… pretending we'd changed places. She has my rooms at home…they're in a wing by themselves built out over the garden. So she used to write me…such good letters…and sign them Susan.

(OLIVER *comes in.*)

OLIVER: Morning. Morning, Susan.

SUSAN: Good morning, Oliver.

(OLIVER *picks up the railway guide from the table and turns the pages. later he sits and unlocks a drawer for some money.*)

ELEANOR: (*To* SUSAN) If you wouldn't mind waiting at the Ministry when I see Mr Pemberton…then we could go straight on to Poplar. They'll give us lunch at the factory. I must be back and at Grosvenor Road by two-thirty. I'll get my papers.

SUSAN: Very well.

ELEANOR: This is shocking news, Oliver.

OLIVER: Very.

(ELEANOR *goes.* SUSAN *looks across at* OLIVER.)

SUSAN: Don't you care?

OLIVER: Yes. What good will that do?

SUSAN: Some good to you.

OLIVER: I wasn't thinking of my own moral improvement for the moment.

SUSAN: Must we quarrel…even about this?

OLIVER: It's how I show affection for you, Susan.

SUSAN: Thank you. I'd give anything to be with her. How horribly casual you all are. I bring you such news…you all say that you loved her…you go about your business. How is one to learn to like you? I've tried not to seem a sightseer…simply curious about everything. I've tried to forget myself among you and find out what I really cared for.

ELEANOR: (*Off*) Ready, Susan.

OLIVER: Why should you like us, my dear, Susan?

(SUSAN *goes without another word.* OLIVER *goes about his business, after a moment* EVAN *comes back.*)

EVAN: As it happens the boat doesn't sail till three.

OLIVER: The eleven-twenty train will do you, then.

EVAN: They're keeping me a cabin.

OLIVER: You've four hundred odd in current.

EVAN: I'll write to Manning for an overdraft. You can cable another five to New York.

OLIVER: Do you expect to see her alive?

EVAN: Hardly. I'll give you a line for Duddington.

OLIVER: You might just be back for the polling.

EVAN: If Duddington thinks he can get my photograph and the gramophone records elected, he's welcome to try. Or you'd make an excellent member. Say to Stephen I'm sorry.

(By now EVAN *is busy at his table.* EVAN *and* OLIVER *talk while they work.)*

OLIVER: Eleanor's just gone out.

EVAN: Yes.

OLIVER: You won't come back.

EVAN: That's always a possibility.

OLIVER: Why ever are you going? What's the use?

EVAN: None.

OLIVER: Here's the cheque. What about your packing?

EVAN: I'll fill another bag.

OLIVER: Will you cable you're starting?

EVAN: No. *(He goes.)*

(End of Scene)

Scene 2

*(*LORD CLUMBERMERE *is sitting waiting. He is reading a little leather-found pocket volume. The door opens and* SUSAN *enters, with a cablegram in hand.)*

SUSAN: Oh, I'm sorry. Excuse me. I can leave this on the desk…or I'll write Mr Strowde a note.

*(*SUSAN *goes to* OLIVER'*s desk and sits there.* CLUMBERMERE *having risen when she came in, sits back down. She, having taken a sheet of paper, decides not to write. Instead, she puts the cablegram itself into an envelope which she addresses. then, looking up, she finds him looking at her.)*

CLUMBERMERE: You came with Miss Strowde to see round our Garden City. I showed you around. My name is Clumbermere.

SUSAN: Yes. I didn't think you'd remember me.

CLUMBERMERE: You come from America.

SUSAN: Yes.

CLUMBERMERE: That cablegram's bad news. I'm sorry.

(OLIVER *comes in hurriedly, and as if directly from the street.*)

OLIVER: You never got my message, my lord! Your City office said they could find you...I rang up Grosvenor Square as well...and you've been here since three.

CLUMBERMERE: I have.

OLIVER: I'm very sorry. The message was that Mr Strowde couldn't keep the appointment with you...he is sailing this afternoon on the *Aquitania*.

CLUMBERMERE: Sudden.

(*For the first time,* OLIVER *takes a good look at* SUSAN *and sees her face:*)

OLIVER: What's the matter, Susan?

(*In silence* SUSAN *hands* OLIVER *the envelope.*)

OLIVER: She's dead?

SUSAN: Yes.

OLIVER: (*As he opens it*) Please excuse me. (*He reads.*) This has come through quickly. (*Then turns again to* CLUMBERMERE) My uncle thought...I've just left him... you might like to make some suggestion to avoid bringing your business with Mr Strowde to a standstill.

CLUMBERMERE: I know no more than you tell me, of course...if you now want to telephone to Southampton to stop him, there's a line in my office that can be relied on...and it's at your service.

OLIVER: Thank you. The boat sailed at three.

SUSAN: That might mean four.

OLIVER: It might.

CLUMBERMERE: Then the Admiralty wireless will do as well. He could land at Cherbourg.

OLIVER: Yes. You'd rather not see my uncle, of course. His point was that...whenever Mr Strowde did come back the Government's relations to him might have altered.

(CLUMBERMERE *is pleasantly amused at the senatorial tone; but he keeps his secret.*)

CLUMBERMERE: I catch that point.

OLIVER: And if you think the business pressing...?

CLUMBERMERE: I think we had now better let things happen for a little...will you tell your good uncle with my compliments? But say I'm always pleased to talk to a man that has a mind of his own and knows it...when they find another.

OLIVER: I'll say so. And I'm sure Mr Strowde would have wished me to say that he was sorry to leave things in the lurch.

CLUMBERMERE: Well, you know, from one cause and another...accidents and such like...that's always occurring. We just can't help thinking this world won't go on without us...the evidence is that it will. A little differently? Perhaps. Any worse? That's more doubtful. (*Look at* SUSAN) Not that you should feel this way.

SUSAN: Why not?

CLUMBERMERE: You're young. I'm old.

SUSAN: If it's all to make so little difference, why do you work fourteen hours a day, Lord Clumbermere?

CLUMBERMERE: The newspapers say that of me. I don't do more than six hours' real work.

SUSAN: Why do any?

CLUMBERMERE: It's a habit I've got into. It passes the time…keeps me happy…and I don't know what else would.

SUSAN: (*Hesitates, then*) It isn't my business to ask, I know, but…do you want Mr Strowde to come back?

CLUMBERMERE: In a friendly sense?

SUAN Do you think he ought to come back?

CLUMBERMERE: Dear young lady, that pistol is not loaded. It is not my business to say.

SUSAN: I beg your pardon.

(CLUMBERMERE *now takes account of the silent* OLIVER.)

CLUMBERMERE: Am I keeping you and Miss Kittredge from private conversation?

OLIVER: No, I think not.

CLUMBERMERE: For my next appointment is not till four, and I have only a mile and a quarter to walk to it. This is my day for meeting men on their own ground. If I meet them on mine more than four days a week, I find I grow too obstinate.

(OLIVER *can hardly bear this old gentleman.*)

OLIVER: Is that a bad business quality?

CLUMBERMERE: It is an unpleasing human quality.

OLIVER: I thought that the set jaw and the thump on the table were the only sure signs of a strong man.

CLUMBERMERE: Don't you like me?

OLIVER: I'm sorry, sir…if that sounded rude.

CLUMBERMERE: I judged you didn't like me when you came to bring papers to that Amalgamated Plantations meeting last November year...which was the first time I saw you.

OLIVER: It must please people amazingly to find out how well you remember them.

CLUMBERMERE: I hope it does. I mean it to. Will you be out of a job now?

OLIVER: Well, I've hardly had time to consider. Possibly.

CLUMBERMERE: I can offer you one.

OLIVER: A firm offer?

CLUMBERMERE: I make no other kind.

OLIVER: No, thank you, my lord. I've tried the City. I am against you, I fear.

CLUMBERMERE: Is that so? And what are you for?

OLIVER: It's not an easy question to answer, you think?

CLUMBERMERE: I think there's only one way to answer it, Mr Gauntlett...and I doubt if you've had time to find that. Miss Kittredge has her eye on this little volume that I carry in my pocket to occupy odd moments. No, it's not a Testament...though I carry a Testament sometimes. Allow me. Nor a Ready Reckoner. Allow me.

(CLUMBERMERE *hands it to* SUSAN.)

OLIVER: What is it, Susan?

SUSAN: *Everybody's Book of Short Poems.*

CLUMBERMERE: They're poor poems mostly, I should suppose. It was the *Everybody's* caught my fancy just about forty years ago, at Bletchley station, when I was travelling in ink.

OLIVER: Ink for everybody!

CLUMBERMERE: That's what I had to make it if I could.

OLIVER: You did.

CLUMBERMERE: Then bottles, pens, paper, typewriters, rubber, lead mines, and a line of steamships. I have prospered, you may say, by giving people what they want…and then a little more of what they want…and sometimes, maybe, by persuading them to take rather more than they did want. Are you against that?

OLIVER: What do you want, my lord?

CLUMBERMERE: Ah…that's the riddle…and there's a catch in it. There's always a catch in the riddles Life sets us to guess, Mr Gauntlett. I have had to live to find the answer…and I don't say I've found it yet. Now the poem I happened to be reading when Miss Kittredge came in…page sixty-two, I have no literary memory, but I retain numbers…is entitled: "I know that my own will come to me." A helpful thought…but an awful thought. I never supposed I wanted lots of money… but I've got it. I despise titles…I'm a lord. I was bred to the Baptist ministry, and I still think I'm a spiritually minded man. And perhaps if I'd been blessed with three children instead of seven, I might be running a chapel now. You'd say I've sunk my soul…not to mention other people's…all in money and money's worth. Well, money's a hard master…so is success. You think you're all for truth and justice. Right. Come and run my pen factory and find out if that is so.

OLIVER: If I ran your pen factory, I'd be for the pen, the whole pen, and nothing but the pen.

CLUMBERMERE: Then you'd be little use to me. If I want a good gold nib, it's religion we must make it with.

OLIVER: I'm sure that sentiment has been applauded on many a Pleasant Sunday Afternoon.

CLUMBERMERE: It has.

OLIVER: But are you a devil, then, my lord, that you want to beat the souls of men into pen nibs?

CLUMBERMERE: I hope not. But if I am, Mr Gauntlett, please show me the way out of the pit. For I've tried to uplift my fellows...gratis; that was a failure...at five per cent; that wasn't quite such a failure...but it was all a failure really. Odd now. My last turn to with Mr Strowde was on this very subject, when we crossed with a party on the 'Caronia' to a conference upon the scientific management of Industry in Chicago. *(To SUSAN)* You're not from Chicago?

SUSAN: No, I've never been there. I don't know much of America, I fear.

CLUMBERMERE: You are America...you don't need to be too self-conscious. I must have done a hundred miles round the decks coming and going, arguing with him. A fine mind. That's eighteen years ago. I was interested in his future.

OLIVER: Did you offer him the pen factory?

CLUMBERMERE: Why, Mr Gauntlett, I wish to make no comparisons...but I offered him the rubber and the steamships. And I will again if he wants a job.

SUSAN: One for you, Oliver.

OLIVER: Yes.

CLUMBERMERE: But he said he had enough to think about.

OLIVER: You don't despise sheer thinking.

CLUMBERMERE: Why, no. My factories are run by thought.

OLIVER: As well as by faith and honour.

CLUMBERMERE: Yes, I'm greedy for all three. And I get greedier. I sometimes wish I didn't...but I do. Why should the immortal part of man be all used up making him safe and comfortable? It's humiliating. And even the demand for simple goodness is greater than the supply. My business swallows a lot…it could swallow a lot more.

OLIVER: Then do you wonder there are people that want to blow you and your factories to smithereens?

CLUMBERMERE: No, I sympathise. But it isn't practical of them…and it wouldn't be popular…for where should we all be then? Subtracting evil doesn't leave good…. Not as I was taught to do sums. So I must seek salvation the other way?

OLIVER: What is that?

(CLUMBERMERE *looks at his watch; he gets up, and as he takes his little book back:*)

CLUMBERMERE: On page one hundred and twelve… thank you, I wasn't forgetting it…there is a poem entitled "It's the little bit extra that counts for God." A good thought. Righteousness is profit, Mr Gauntlett… and before we can have honest profit we must pay our way. I know that is only the creed of a businessman. It's half-past three…and I'm a slow walker… (*To* SUSAN) Good afternoon.

SUSAN: Could you give me a job?

CLUMBERMERE: I might.

SUSAN: I may come and ask for one.

CLUMBERMERE: Do. My coat's outside. (*He pauses.*) I liked to think when I was beginning to do well that my business was, as you might say, the practical side of literature. Great poems must have been written in my ink…and treaties have been signed with my pens. So's my hat. (*As he goes out, to* OLIVER) Will you tell your uncle then that I think things must be let happen for a little now…till we see a chance to interfere again…

(The door closes on the two of them. but in a moment,
OLIVER *returns—to find* SUSAN *very ready for him.)*

SUSAN: Oliver, why wouldn't you telephone? I thought
he'd stay talking for ever. Don't you mean to send the
wireless?

OLIVER: I don't think so.

SUSAN: Why not? Don't they want him back now?

*(*OLIVER *can let himself go at last; and what's more, he can
take it out on* SUSAN.*)*

OLIVER: Did they ever want him here? They hated
him, they were afraid of him, they're thankful to be
rid of him and they're furious he's gone. Poor Uncle
Stephen…I caught him at Downing Street…and his
temper for once did run out like a line with a fish at
the end of it. You should hear Henry Chartres over the
telephone. Stop and see Eleanor's face when I tell her.
Then there's Duddington, his election agent…he'll be
here soon.

SUSAN: But why don't you want him back?

OLIVER: *(Scornfully)* He threw away a seat in the
Cabinet, did he, just to go and cry at her bedside? But
now it's too late he's to dodge back thanking God she
didn't wait to die till he was well out on the Atlantic.
Don't be so materially minded, my dear, even if you
are a sentimentalist.

SUSAN: I didn't say I thought it right his going at all. I
hadn't an idea he'd gone.

OLIVER: What a wife you'll make some day, Susan, for
a successful man.

SUSAN: What's the precise point of that, please?

OLIVER: Spartan, but accommodating. Ever ready to
indicate the practical ideal.

SUSAN: What's to happen to this world if people won't choose their duty and stick to it though their hearts break?

OLIVER: Yes, you've the patter quite pat. Good girl... trailing with your notebook at Eleanor's heels too... giving Clumbermere and Co marks for their interest in Social Welfare. And she's not been looking so glum lately at the wicked party politicians round the lunch table.

SUSAN: She's been glad to see him busy again...and happy.

OLIVER: Busy and happy...oh, what more is there to be. *(He even takes a turn at what he thinks is a most American phrase)* And isn't it just 'too wonderful' to have the great men that govern the great British Empire feeding off the very next plate!

SUSAN: *(Angry)* Will you send that wireless?

OLIVER: No...let him go... He was glad to go.

SUSAN: Do you mean to torture him for a week with the doubt if he'll find her alive?

(SUSAN wins a point, OLIVER owns up.)

OLIVER: Ah...you have me there. Smart Susan.

SUSAN: Isn't it for him to say now whether he'll come back or not?

OLIVER: Yes. He won't.

SUSAN: I'm sure he will.

(OLIVER considers this, and with a touch of exhaustion:)

OLIVER: There's time enough. If I go down to the Admiralty I can actually talk to him. I'll take you. You can tell him in a hushed voice...not too hushed, and it'll be a bit broken by the buzzing...that Joan has...

passed over, is the pretty phrase, isn't it…and will he please come back and forget her….

SUSAN: Oh…it's been nothing but an afternoon's delight to you…the destruction of his going. This talk about everything, and nothing said about anything. I think that silly old man was quite right about you, Oliver…and you don't know what you want.

OLIVER: There's a worse mischief with most of us, Susan. What we do want doesn't count. We want money and we want peace…and we want our own way. Some of us want things to look beautiful and some want to be good. And Clumbermere gets rich without knowing why…and we statesmen sit puzzling how best to pick his pocket. And you want Evan to come back to the muddle of it all. I'll go to the Admiralty.

SUSAN: I'll wait for Eleanor.

(*Stopping* OLIVER:)

SUSAN: Why didn't Joan marry him? They'd have had some happiness at least…and that would have helped.

OLIVER: Why doesn't life plan out into pretty patterns and happy endings?

SUSAN: Don't mock at me, Oliver. If she loved him she should have married him.

OLIVER: Love isn't all of that sort. Sometimes it brings Judgement Day… (*He goes.*)

(*Leaving* SUSAN *alone.*)

(*End of Scene*)

Scene Three

(Two days earlier. We see the corner by the window of
SUSAN'*s little sitting room at Countesbury, Massachusetts.*
It is a white room; and now the snow outside makes it seem
even whiter still. And the snow brings with it a silence
too. JOAN, *wrapped in shawls, is tucked into an armchair.*
KITTREDGE *is sitting next to her. Her eyes are closed, she*
might be dead. When she speaks she does not open them at
first. And she never moves, at most a hand reaches out.)

JOAN: So white. And white now even when I shut my
eyes.

KITTREDGE: No pain then?

JOAN: None since this morning, thank you.

KITTREDGE: We are wise children when we fear the
dark.

JOAN: Yes…now that I don't sleep much at night time,
I'm learning how to lose myself to light. What more
has dear Susan to say?

KITTREDGE: I had finished the letter.

JOAN: Stupid of me.

KITTREDGE: Did you doze?

JOAN: I slipped out through the window…into the
snow. I wonder if I've been a very wicked woman.

KITTREDGE: Probably not…if you wonder.

JOAN: I'd have been so content to be nothing but a wife
and a mother…a link in the chain. In our pedigree book
at home there's an Edward Marshall, knight, not so
far back, that married…two little dashes…Eliza. Plain,
simple Eliza. Who was she? Scandalous mystery…no
one wanted to remember. But I've always felt tenderly
and dutifully towards my great, great, great…and
then, after all, one loses count…great grandmother

Eliza. (*Pause*) Such a bright, silent land. Do you love it as we love England? Not yet. It's harder. It doesn't look back yet and seem to love you...as England does.

KITTREDGE: It must take more toll of us first perhaps.

JOAN: So many generations of the souls and bodies of men to be given to this earth to breed it a soul of its own. (*Short pause*) My old world has a kindly soul... with a farm and a church and a house with its garden to show for it. I don't think I want to believe, though, that your quiet spirit must pass into the clatter of cities...or is that a music to you with meaning?

KITTREDGE: With no clear meaning. I watch the new generations giving themselves to strange tremendous forces to breed...what sort of a monster world.

JOAN: I was very scared sailing up the harbor to New York and driving to the station. Those blasphemous towers of Babel weren't a bit like you. But I think you'll come out on top. Yes...I have a vision of the sublime you, conscious, persistent, wise...coming out truly on top. (*Short pause*) Harry, till he was ten, poor infant, had dreadful headaches...and he asked me once, Mother, am I good? So I said he was. Then he asked, need he pray for eternal life? For if it's going to hurt like this, he said, I don't see how I could bear it.

KITTREDGE: I wish I'd known Harry.

JOAN: I wish he'd known you in time. Some of those boys, under the shadow of death, came suddenly to a maturity of mind.

KITTREDGE: This world at least was theirs. What a gift to them.

JOAN: You're seldom bitter.

KITTREDGE: Too seldom. I dread the vapid benevolence of old age.

JOAN: Better the pain of anger? *(Short pause)* I have the shamefullest sin to confess…a sin of being. I have treasured a secret self…oh, an ego, if ever there was one.

KITTREDGE: A tyrant.

JOAN: Too aloof and alone for tyranny.

KITTREDGE: Lonely?

JOAN: Never so human. It doesn't age, it doesn't suffer…and now I've lain awake with it so much I doubt if it ever sleeps. So I have this dread that it's undying.

KITTREDGE: I once knew a promising young man possessed of the same devil. He fell in love, had his heart broken…broken into. Ego came out to fight and could never quite get back again.

JOAN: How vulgar…says my secret self, and sniffs. No, I could never flatter it into being a heart-breaker. It was never half so human. May I confess?

KITTREDGE: Will my absolution serve?

JOAN: Give it me of your wisdom and your kindness if you can. Once, I the sheer place of my self's refuge, I found that I was not alone. I turned back to life for safety. We loved the unattainable in each other, so we said…and were content to part. When there was no more need for parting we found that it was true. A faith was born in us…a dead faith…to my shame. And I left him to bear its burden. The world he worked for had much hope for him…and need of him.

KITTREDGE: And he failed it?

JOAN: He let life go. He worked on…lifelessly. Better if we had disbelieved.

KITTREDGE: There's no doing that.

JOAN: Why had I no power to bring the faith that kindled to a living birth…to set it free…that we might serve it? I hadn't….that was the worst. The sacred self that cannot yield to life. Let's only hope the soul's as mortal as the body is… *(Pain)*

KITTREDGE: Your head is hurting you again.

JOAN: Beginning to.

KITTREDGE: Take my hand.

JOAN: Thank you…that's comforting.

KITTREDGE: We must be patient…with headaches. The first discovery, do you know, of my imaginative life was to find a story coming to an unhappy end and to hide the book away with its last chapter still unread. But suddenly that small boy thought: No story ever ends. A very moral anecdote. *(Pain)* Grip my hard hand…and I'll grip yours harder.

JOAN: Please.

KITTREDGE: I've written a book or two on ethics…. Unfinished stories in their kin… Maybe what I've best learned how to do by that is to sit here…

JOAN: Be stern with me…or I can't bear it, I'm afraid.

KITTREDGE: Headache or heartache or a harder thing… those that can suffer them must suffer them, it seems. You are the stuff, Joan, that forges well.

JOAN: I am learning a way, I think. Will you tell him, please, that as the light grows there's always a moment he's with me…till it grows too dazzling.

KITTREDGE: I'll tell him…

JOAN: I've cut your hand with my ring.

KITTREDGE: Good. I have shed my blood for you.

JOAN: Thank you.

KITTREDGE: Keep the head still now. There is an Eastern prayer…for those that would leave life behind… begins: From the need to know by name and by form… deliver me.

JOAN: Oh, I like that! *(Pause)* Yesterday you told me that three times in your life you had been near to…it was a deserter's phrase…

KITTREDGE: Yes…three times…no more. Good friends, clean enemies, and hard work have kept me happy mostly.

JOAN: What held you in place?

KITTREDGE: Inconsequent things. Once, it was the thought of an unfinished book that had been paid for. Once, a night's sleep made all the difference. But once my self-respect did seriously protest against a premature indulgence of death.

JOAN: Did the troubles pass?

KITTREDGE: No. They were unsolved problems. I face them still.

(Pause)

JOAN: I was in London this morning…it was full of cheerful noise. And yesterday I was in camp again beyond Khartoum…watching the little black babies crawl about the sand. I can remember one that died and didn't want to die…he fought the air with his fists…

(Silence)

END OF PLAY

THE HERITAGE OF THE ACTOR
An Essay by Harley Granville Barker *(1923)*

A play is material for acting. It may be far more, but it must be that to begin with. The actor brings it to a technical completion. This, no doubt, puts the matter from the actor's point of view, and while the truth is indisputable, the emphasis of the statement may be misleading. Even so, this point of view counts; if only because, when we bring a play to the theatre, the actor's is the last word in the matter—till the public has its say. If it be argued that the play is implicitly complete when it leaves the author's hands, that the actor's business is interpretation merely, that he can, in truth, add nothing to and take nothing away from the material a competent playwright has given him—

There was once, in the 17th century, a gentleman, who, coming out of church on a Sunday morning, found a week-day companion sitting in the stocks.

'"What have they put you there for?" he asked.

'"Getting drunk."

'"Nonsense," said the church-goer, who was a legally-minded man; "they can't put you in the stocks for being drunk."

'"Zooks!" said the unfortunate reveller. "But they *have!*"'

It is useless to argue that actors can add nothing to and
take nothing from the material the playwright gives
them. The answer is that they do.

This final part of the dramatic process, this putting
of a play upon the stage, is, indeed, a distressingly
incalculable thing. Certainly it is interpretation, but
no other kind of interpretation quite compares with
it. Musicians have instruments that are more or less
mechanical to perform on; even singers are tied, stave
by stave, to definite notes. Singers and players will tell
us, however, that they should be left ample discretion.
They may add that the meticulous method of writing
music is quite modern, that composers of the 18th
century and earlier were content to put down on paper
what they considered the essentials, and to leave far
more to the artistry of their interpreters.

But let any one familiar with play production ask
himself what the final effect would be if the actors
felt called upon to do no more than speak a speech
as the author was good enough to pronounce it to
them, trippingly upon the tongue. A certain regardless
beauty might result. There are plays that, at first
thought, would seem to profit by this treatment. Greek
tragedy, with its use of mask and cothurnus, asks
for its acting a voice and a presence, and little else;
though, even so, it may be found that concentration
upon this single means of expression rather heightens
than diminishes a personality that *can* so express itself.
But in a play which pictures human intercourse in
accustomed terms, if the actor did not do something
more than repeat its words with such understanding
and emotion as they immediately suggested to him,
pointing them with appropriate gesture, the result
would be unbearably flat and quite unconvincing.

What, then, is the 'something more' he is expected
to contribute? His personality. What, then, is the

extension of this in the terms of his art to be? Drama
ranges from the austerity of Greek tragedy to the
freedom of the Commedia dell' Arte; and it is not for
one manifestation of it, however respectable, however
popular, to deny the validity of any other. The antics
of Harlequin are not essentially different from the
art that shows us Œdipus. But, to bring the question
to a practical and a more or less topical issue, let us
rule out both drama that is largely ritual and drama
that is inchoate. Let us assume a play conceived by an
author in essential completeness, and marked down for
interpretation as minutely as words will do it.

There is a story of an actress of genius who was
being conducted through a rehearsal of her part by a
producer of great ability. 'Miss ——,' he said, 'you go
here and there and here; and you do this and that and
this.' 'Thank you,' she replied, with perfect docility.
'Yes, I think I understand. I go there and here and
there, and I do that and this and that. And then I do
the little bit extra, don't I, for which you really pay me
my salary?' Or, as she might have put it, even more
informingly, 'Then I *am* the little bit extra which no one
can teach me to be.'

The dramatist has a right to expect that any actor, of
the required sex and of the right age and appearance
—picked out of a list, called off the rank as it were—
will be able to say and do with perfect efficiency
whatever can be set down for him to say and do. This
right, like many others, is often in abeyance. But,
with the expectation fulfilled, the dramatist will still
ask the actor to *be* something besides. At times, no
doubt, this 'being' is offensive. We have all seen plays
swamped by an elaborate exhibition of some one
personality. We have, on the other hand, seen plays of
the poorest sort enriched beyond recognition by the
imposition—as upon one of those vague backgrounds

used by Victorian photographers—of vivid characters, springing, if not from the imagination of the actors of them, then from where? Irving's Mathias will certainly not be found in the original manuscript of 'The Bells.' And if one is to be told that it was in some mysterious fashion innate in the story and the play as Erckmann-Chatrian and the adapter wrote them, one must ask further: was Coquelin's conception of the innkeeper-murderer innate there too? If so, the authors had an uncommonly accommodating or a somewhat divided mind.

The dramatist demands personality; an indefinable thing, and, alas, he is seldom content with the concrete specimen of it that he gets. It is amusing to watch him at rehearsal while he sees the characters growing quite unlike his own innocent idea of them. If he is altogether a novice, the fascination of seeing them live and move is usually sufficient compensation. But novelists turned playwrights are apt to be agonised by the phenomenon. Experience—and a little sympathy with the difficulties of the actor—will teach them how what is essential may be kept alive and true to the play's purpose if incidentals are not rigidly insisted on. Does the author refuse to admit any such division? Authors, grown expert enough in the whole business to instruct each actor to a nicety, have been known to do so. They make their choice, then, between the letter and the spirit, and they may find that by insistence upon the letter they have—for sensitive auditors at least—taken away the very life of the play's performance.

Not but that the author may suffer in a hundred ways by an actor's freedom to inform his part with life. I can myself recall a performance in which an actor—well-intentioned too—gave what was rather a destructive criticism than a representation of the character he was playing. The author thought he had written a not

unsympathetic hero. The actor proved conclusively
to the audience that the fellow was nothing of the
kind. He may have been right; but the author could
not unreasonably have remarked that there were
critics enough in the stalls and that it was not an
actor's business to do their work for them. Reverse the
process; let the actor take a sordid character and invest
it with distinction and charm, and still the author is
not grateful. He will prefer the child of his fancy to this
changeling, even though the changeling be a fairy. The
work of the modern theatre, however, where authors
and actors of average ability are concerned, is done,
as a whole, upon the basis of a compromise by which
the author provides essentials and the actor incidentals
to taste. That modern invention, the producer, is
the honest broker brought in to effect it. It answers,
doubtless; and the bulk of the work done under it may
be pleasing enough. But is there no more to be said?
For there is no future in a compromise.

And the theatre finds itself to-day, not in any more
trouble than usual (*It is always in trouble*), but facing a
curiously ambiguous outlook for the future. For two
things have happened recently in England. Every
one has learned to read, almost every one has taken
to reading fiction (*Some of it disguised, as fact!*). And
the Cinema has become an institution. The first event
did not rob the theatre of its devotees; there was no
reason that it should. Theatre-going is a social act,
though in England less so regarded than elsewhere;
and the enjoyment of narrative is no good substitute
for the excitement of mimic action. But cinema-going
is a social act too, and—'Movies'; the very word spells
action and excitement. Now it is too soon to say—it
will always be too soon to say—how the art of the
cinema may develop. There is no reason to suppose
that, as industries, theatre and cinema cannot exist side

by side, for the theatre has many resources *(As we shall argue)* that the cinema can hardly draw upon. But it is fairly certain that the story in action—that extension of the narrative fiction, for which such a widespread taste has been cultivated—will remain the cinema's chief aim, and that the theatre therefore will tend to be ousted from this part of its ancient preserve.

It is instructive to examine the cinema's dealing with material that has been or well might be used by the theatre. There is, very naturally, a revolt from the unities, from that 'general oneness' so dear to the heart of Mr Curdle—and Aristotle. Continuity of action, with the variety attendant upon it, is favoured as against the elaborate development of particular episodes. In so far, indeed, as the cinema is disposed to lean on dramatic technique at all, it returns rather to the cruder methods of the Elizabethan, even of the Mediæval stage. Little is left for the imagination to account for. It is as if the scientific discovery, by which the swiftly revolving shutter makes the pictures appear to move, had laid down artistic law. The story is chopped up into little pieces, then cemented again into a long episodic line. The cinema has certainly revived the Mediæval dumb-show and our delight in it.

It is specially instructive to note, when a play is transferred to the screen, how much dialogue can be eliminated without peril to our understanding, or even to our enjoyment of the story. The skill of the producer is very properly directed to removing what—the picture being now the thing—has become mere excrescence. It follows that plays which depend upon poetry, upon wit, upon analysis of character, are very weak vessels in the eye—in the brilliantly winking eye—of the camera. And, if there are degrees in the matter, this is truest of poetry, our great begetter of emotion in the theatre. The cinema deals in excitement;

only by indirect means does it beget emotion. Hence, no doubt, its invariable accompaniment by music, for an arbitrary stimulus to the feelings.

As an entertainment the cinema has one further difference; it asks no response from its audience. Go to a play, and unless you are insensitive indeed, you will be drawn to some sympathy with the actors. It may take the form of admiration (*The form, no doubt, that actors prefer*), it may be reduced to mere pity for fellow-creatures making such fools of themselves. But in some form or other it will be there. You will, if you analyse your feelings, be brought to some sense of responsibility for the conduct of the entertainment as a whole. An exhibition of giggling bad manners by one of your neighbours can easily put this to a test. If you do not protest, you will at least feel ashamed.

But, watching a 'Movie,' what does its foolishness matter? The actors are far away, both in space and in time. What consideration need be shown to their flickering images on a screen? Equally, what enthusiasm can such images arouse, except in the minds of children (*Of whatever age*) to whom illusion still is life and the discretionary enjoyment of art a thing unknown? This environment of irresponsibility may add to the cinema's popularity in an irresponsible age. But one doubts whether an art that cannot stimulate emotion and that asks for no more judgment or support from its audience than is involved in their paying or not paying, their staying or going, can ever take a very deep hold. One might even find refuge in fogeyism and question its right in the outcome—whatever æsthetic efforts may be spent in preparation—to be considered an art at all. But, art or no art, if the cinema is in the future to steal some part of the theatre's thunder, what had the theatre best do about it? We see well enough how the industrial part of the question is being answered. Landlords, dramatists, and actors are putting money in their purses while they can. What preparation, though, is the indisputable art of the drama making for a generation that is perhaps growing up to think of a play in relation to a Movie as the children of 1880, riding in express trains, thought of a coach-and-four?

If an art may have a policy it would seem as if the first thing needful were the envisaging of what the drama can do unapproachably, of what it can be at its best that neither kindred arts nor pseudo-arts can be. For in this must lie its strength to face a future, however ambiguous. Its history has been marked by defections, from which, in some ways it has gathered strength. Dancing and music deserted, to set up on their own account as ballet and opera. Drama on the whole does better without them. Certainly, late in the 17th century it struck up one doubtful alliance with the scenic art, by which it has benefited a little and suffered a lot; the Artist *(With a capital A)* being a difficult partner to keep in his place, once he has scented the footlights, and an appeal to the thing seen being ever the simplest to make. Four boards and a passion, it has been said, are all the equipment that drama needs, and it is a saying to be taken to heart. Here are the things that drama has never surrendered; her unrivalled riches. First, the fellowship set up between actors and audience on the strength of the fellowship of imagination between the actors themselves. Next, the power of the spoken word. And in these two things the power and the quality of the art must lie.

Now it is worth noting, incidentally, that the final framing-in of the picture stage *(Which preceded by a generation the invention of 'the pictures')* led in time to the loss of that emotional intimacy by which our 'classic' drama had re-inforced doubly and trebly its

poetry and humour. The discovery of the loss was
tardy; partly because the poetic play and 18th-century
comedy dropped out of fashion just then, partly
because actors of authority, who knew what the old
ways were, adapted them skilfully enough to the new
conditions. Even so there was much critical mourning
over Macbeths that were not what they used to be, and
Schools for Scandal as dull as ditchwater.

This is worth noting because it points so directly to
the reliance once placed—apart from any virtues in
the play itself—upon the relation between actors and
audience. This relation bred (*unfortunately for the drama
as a whole perhaps*) a race of actors who, by cultivating
it, could make the very poorest play attractive—even
as a music-hall comedian can now keep his audience in
a roar over nothing at all. But, aesthetically, it was not
of necessity an unworthy relation. No one can read of
Garrick and Mrs Siddons and Kean; of King and Mrs
Abington and Palmer; no one can have seen a William
Farren play Sir Peter Teazle according to tradition,
and suppose so. And it would be idle to pretend that
in erecting the barrier of a complete illusion between
actors and audience the art of the theatre has lost
nothing, whatever it may have gained. The arising of
a generation of actors that feel as helpless upon the
apron at Garrick's Drury Lane (*Which just from the
actor's standpoint keeps all the advantage of Shakespeare's
Globe*) as they would in the ring of a circus, will involve
the disappearance of Shakespeare and Sheridan
from the stage, except as excuses for pageantry or
academic exercises. This disappearance has indeed
seemed imminent; it still may be. Here and there the
mechanical remedy has been applied, when old plays
are under treatment, of breaking down the illusion by
providing an apron stage and encouraging the actor to

come out upon it and 'be a Garrick,' so to speak. But the trouble may not be quite so simply curable.

And what of the modern drama? It is as useless to expect the playwright of to-day to go back on the 'illusionary' theory as it would be to ask Mr Sargent to paint like Giotto. Besides, this would be to imply that in the illusionary stage we have nothing to be grateful for. We have much. One need not muster names, or even suppose that the playwrights who have flourished during the last fifty years and whose work measures up in average quality with any the theatre has seen could not have done as well—though they must have done very differently—working to another technique. The 'could' and 'should' argument in matters of art is always exasperatingly futile, whether it bears on the past or the present; whether, as in this instance, it is how Shakespeare ought to have written for footlights and scenery, or Ibsen might have constructed Hedda Gabler for the bare boards of the Globe.

But it will be owned that this latest period of development in drama has been the playwright's period, not the actor's. Has it not often brought actor and playwright to odds, now openly, now—for good reasons of bread-and-butter—as politely as you please? Once, at a public dinner, Ibsen was congratulated upon the magnificent parts his plays provided for their interpreters. The old gentleman scowled terrifically. 'Parts!' he said, when he rose to speak; 'I do not write parts. I create men and women.' On the other hand, could the talk of actors gathered together at many a private dinner during the last forty years be recorded, it would rise to Heaven as the discordant wail of a crushed and desolated race.

The quarrel, I repeat, may seldom be particularised. A theatre is the happiest of workshops and its controllers

have to learn that happiness is a necessary part of
its efficiency. And, as I have suggested, in practice
these conflicting interests are accommodated by a
compromise. Let there be so much sheer interpretation
of the part I have written, so much exploiting, my dear
Mr So-and-so, of your personality. Never, of course,
is it put in so many words, or even thought of with so
brutal a clarity. And where the domination of either
author or producer on the one hand, or of actor on the
other, is perfect and unquestioned, no overt difference
will be detected. The author murmurs approvingly
from the shrouded stalls, or the actors obediently note
that they are not only to do but to feel this and that and
no more. Five minutes—five seconds!—at a rehearsal
or performance will tell the experienced observer
which regime is in force. Some rehearsals, doubtless,
run their course upon a basis of conflict to a goal of
haphazard performance. If the play is a success—
and good plays and bad plays, bad performances of
them and good ones, succeed and fail equally—no
one concerned asks any questions. If it is a failure,
the author feels, 'Ah, if *my play* had had a chance . . .!'
and the actors either 'Ah, if I'd only had something
to act . . .!' or 'If they'd only have let me *act* it!' It is a
stupid quarrel. And what is its result, in ensuing or
suppression, for the playgoer? That good actors often
prefer bad plays; and that good plays are too often
deplorably badly acted.

If this is the dramatist's day, he will be wise to consider
the actor, not as a mere appendage to his work, but as
its very life-giver. Let him realise that the more he can
learn to ask of the actor the more will he gain for his
play. But asking is giving. He must give opportunity.

An author may have a thesis to expound or an exciting
story to tell. A pamphlet will serve him for one and a
novel for the other; or if the matter be all excitement,

there is, as aforesaid, the cinema. A play has far
other, far wider, artistic purposes. Aristotle laid it
down—with that positiveness which in an ancient
Greek is supposed, for some reason, to silence all
argument—that dramatic action must not be thought
of with a view to the representation of character, that
the incidents and plot are the end of a tragedy; and the
end is the chief thing of all. To prove this, apparently,
he further remarks that without action there cannot be
a tragedy *(Which is obviously true)*, but that there may
be without character. In some logical sense, no doubt,
there may—and a very dull affair it would be. But
perhaps wise playwrights do not read their Aristotle,
lest they should be in danger of having to differ from
him. For they will remember that every great play of
the last three centuries and more holds its place in
virtue of character and not of plot. Why do we go to
see a play that we really like again and again? *(And
return visits are the test; in music, in painting, in drama.)*
Not to have the story re-told us, however ingeniously
it may be told. It is the elucidation of character that
does not pall; and it is in this—all virtuosity, all that
is learnable allowed for—that the actor's art finds its
final task and its true achievement. As with the actor,
so with the playwright; construction and the rest of
it are as learnable as is good speaking and the tricks
of painting the face; but either he can create men and
women in terms of dramatic action or he cannot. And
nothing else finally counts. He need not, however,
with Ibsen, disdain to think of them as parts to be
played. That was in its time, perhaps, a wholesome
protest against the actor's egoism. But it has become—
frankly—a piece of snobbery and no more. For now as
always it is the power of the actor, adopting the speech
and action of the author's imagining, to elucidate the
character in the terms of his own personality that gives

the thing that apparent spontaneity of life which is the drama's peculiar virtue.

We speak most appropriately of *reviving* an old play; and new actors do in a very real sense give it new life. The fact that *(If it has been, to begin with, vitally conceived)* it is capable of being interpreted in the terms of another set of personalities *(As indeed it may be to some degree variously treated by the same actors time after time)* is the chief reason why we can go back to it, not merely as we go back to a familiar novel or poem, but often to receive—though expectancy is rash—a fresher, more vivid enjoyment than that which it first gave us. It is said in the theatre that no actor ever quite fails as Hamlet. That is truer than it sounds; moreover, it goes far to tell us why Hamlet is the most popular play in the world, not so much with actors, who can indeed fail quite sufficiently in it to be chary of the risk, but with the ever-changing, never-changing public. Popular plays are plays that 'act well.' And the better a play and the better a part the more can an actor find to do in it, and the greater variety of acting will it accommodate.

Modern drama, the actor may tell us, does not give him the chances that the old did. But in much of it there is more for him to do than he is apt to think. For he thinks of great acting too often in terms of the past; his mind stalks that apron-stage of Garrick's. Or, worse, he thinks of it *in vacuo*. His secret heart asks for a play which shall be but a colourable preparation and excuse for his doing something emotionally tremendous. He wants to 'capture' his audience, he yearns *(quite rightly)* after that emotional intimacy with them which will bring them to crying when he gives the cue and laughing when he laughs, without ever asking the reason why. His instinct tells him indeed that the less reason has to do with it the more satisfying his job will

be. Set him free, he feels, to appeal to the hearts of the
people and all will be well. Again, he is right from his
point of view. All *will* be well enough for that moment
of triumph; and he is not responsible for the after-
questionings of an audience convalescent from their
attack of this Dionysiac disease. What was it all about?
That has to be the author's concern; and *he* may—or
may not—have a reputation for sanity which he cares
to preserve.

In the day of the dramatist, therefore, the actor must
not seek that sort of emancipation. He must—it is
the only way in art—break to new liberty through
fulfilment. Modern plays make demands on him that,
he may often think, are less in degree than he deserves;
but, as he may even oftener omit to notice, these differ
almost in kind from the old demands. Until he has
exhausted the possibilities there are he cannot justly
reproach—well, he will not wisely reproach—the
authors of his histrionic being (*If now they have the whip
hand of him*) with not providing more.

This is one side of the matter. Incidentally, we should
never be angry, or even amused, if the actor, once the
play is delivered to him, seems to look on it for the
time being as so much personal adornment. Off the
stage (*If he is ever off the stage*) he generally doesn't; he
is as often too humble-minded. On the stage, better
really encourage him to do so. Assumption of character
is a difficult business. It involves a quite desperate
abandonment of self, a loosing hold of self-confidence,
and a touch of arrogance may be a help and a little
comfort. Certainly the actor whose performance is
but a deferential protest that all this is really more the
author's affair than his, is not worth his salt.

The modern dramatist's side of the case begins with a
justification, but ends, it may be, with a question. His
demands on the actor do differ greatly from the old

demands, and the actor has been slow to recognise it.
One need not here try to trace the process of change.
In such matters the march is often enough two steps
forward to one back and to several sideways. But the
landmark which divides past from present is a change
in the convention of illusion; and from this, once
made, change after change has sprung. Plays can be
found that straddle the boundary; drama may come to
recrossing it, or may pass on over another; it is possible
to argue the difference away. But the plain fact is that
the writer of to-day, setting himself to mirror some
fraction of contemporary life in dramatic form, goes
to work under technical obligations that a century ago
could have found no application at all, that fifty years
back were but emerging from the tangle of an older,
a much worn tradition. If they are not to be stated
in a phrase or in a dozen phrases, they are none the
less obvious. One might try, not quite successfully,
to round them in with a paradox by saying that the
footlights which symbolise the illusion of the picture
stage now destroy the very division between actors
and audience that they first made. Drama's aim
has not changed. This is still to create an emotional
intimacy between these two; only the means to the
end have shifted, have indeed finally been reversed.
For—paradox apart—by the old method the stage and
the actor were brought into the midst of the audience,
by the new the audience is lured in imagination on
the stage; if it can be hypnotised, even, into forgetting
that such a thing as a stage exists, so much the better.
Wherefore the 'realistic setting' has been perfected.
We have rooms that we may regard as our own, fires
that crackle, lights that our fingers twitch to turn up or
down, doors that shut and bang with a familiar sound.
It is interesting to remember that the end of 'The Doll's
House'—of the play which began this movement—was
the banging of a door.

To such realism naturally belongs realism, or—if one
rejects that abused word—verisimilitude of speech
and action and of the drawing of character generally.
Now, cause and effect in the development of an art
are hard to distinguish. Let us only say then, that
these things have in turn been the occasion of a great
change of content in plays. The actor must follow
where the dramatist leads. Here he has hung back,
he has protested, and he has had times of real and
times of false enthusiasm for the new thing. He has
often succeeded in coaxing the dramatist aside for
an old-fashioned frolic. But, on the main path, he has
had to follow. And the dramatist—this might be his
protest—now puts him in a world which is sometimes
far too like the real one to be at all amusing. He is
expected to know what a bishop, a stockbroker,
a politician, a Frenchman, a Lincolnshire farmer,
or a Scottish professor really are like. He is asked,
moreover, to devote himself, even by the complete
suppression of himself, to exhibiting the commonplace
and expounding the abstruse, not to murmur if, when
the exhibiting and expounding suffices the purpose
of the play, *he* is bundled unceremoniously out of it,
not to complain if he can only find in the paper the
next morning that 'the performance was adequate.'
No wonder he thinks enviously of Edmund Kean and
of 'loud applause' punctuating every few lines of a
performance, and of the days when a Mercutio, after
departing to die, promptly returned to bow to the
cheering, while Romeo and the rest stood around and
the play itself waited his triumph's pleasure.

A generation of actors has already grown up, perhaps,
that takes its new leading-strings for granted;
otherwise the consequent question would be put
more insistently than it is. I will try to put it. Has the
dramatist, busy reconstituting his own art to gain full

advantage from this theatre of the new illusion, given enough thought to all that the art of the actor has to gain from it? Has, in fact, the art of the actor gained in these days of the dramatist's dominance? And, if not, must not any gain to drama itself be but a very partial gain?

There has lately been revolt against verisimilitude. The dramatists themselves look round for ways of emancipation. But the revolt has been led — oddly enough—not by the actor but by designers of scenery. The actor would have been wise to make the quarrel his own and to make it a quarrel of principle. His is the case, but he has let the best of it go to snatch petty advantages here and there. And the scene designer fights, not in his interest at all, but against him.

This revolt against dry verisimilitude was bound to come. Objective truth is well enough; but without emotion and the beauty that springs from it, the theatre simply cannot continue to exist. Ibsen, the great protagonist of serious social drama, was a genius and a poet to boot; and in his later plays the poet is found bursting the bonds of the form the playwright has perfected. But of his followers, not many have been either geniuses or poets, and their work has often been dull—conscientious, but dull. And now we have the scene designer, and even the engineer of the electric light, raising the banner of beauty for beauty's sake, and promising to restore to the theatre all the romantic glory it has lost with increase a thousandfold, if we will but surrender ourselves to their spell-binding, and if actor and dramatist both, like good little boys, will do as they are bid.

It is a strange claim. Ibsen and Shakespeare in the shades must wonder indeed when it comes echoing to them that, for their work to have full value for the theatre, it must be made 'expressionistic.' Actors,

remembering their great predecessors, must feel
a little bored when they are recommended to be
'presentational,' or to wear masks, or, on occasion, to
abdicate altogether in favour of marionettes. Already
we have had 'Macbeth' and 'Richard III' interpreted
by scenic symbolism—which riveted the audience's
attention no doubt, kept people awake wondering
what they'd see next. But the actor of Macbeth must
have reflected somewhat earlier in the play than is
usual, that life was indeed but a walking shadow,
and that he, perhaps, was an idiot as well as a poor
player to be spending his sound and fury against such
odds. 'Hamlet' with the Prince of Denmark left out is
too good a joke not to be taken in earnest sometime.
Are we to have a company of mere human beings
revolving round some mighty symbol of morbid
indecision; a pillar of light, it might be, registering
moods by ranging through the spectrum, with a little
music to help?

Seriously, there are more appropriate—would it be
rude to say saner?—ways of restoring emotion and
beauty to the drama. But unless they are sought for,
we shall continue to be fascinated and bamboozled by
this sort of thing. Scenery has its place in the theatre,
and a sufficiently honourable one. Quite excusably,
men of talent who devote themselves to its designing
will spread their wings and test their power to its
limits. But let them either leave plays and acting out of
account altogether, let them, indeed, practise a new art
of their own; or let them, their flights over, return to
the bedrock fact, that the function of scenery is to be a
background for the play's interpreter, the actor. This is
its place, and, finally, it must be content to stay there.

The beauty of sublimated human emotion; that is the
beauty which properly pertains to drama. Without
this and its complements of wit and humour, drama

will die, and neither brains in the playwright nor the splashing of paint will avail to save it. But there is no need whatever to suppose that the technique of the modern play of verisimilitude is outworn or that its gains to the dramatist must be abandoned in a search for beauty and emotional power. And the gain to drama itself will be entire if the actor can be brought to contribute more largely from his own peculiar resources, the resources of human emotion. Not how to stifle or supersede this in the name of his own new freedom, but how to employ it to new and to subtler purpose should be the dramatist's problem. But—this must be recognised—it is the problem of a partnership. It will not be solved under the tyranny of dramatist or actor. In the lack of a fruitful recognition of this the scene designer has come thrusting in where really he has no business. His interference has resulted in a most beneficent improvement of bad scenery into good. But, if it is to be a question of the development of drama itself—no, no; let him mind his paint-pots.

We may sense what is wrong, yet wisely be chary of dogmatising upon its putting right. Certainly it is futile to request dramatists to give actors better chances of acting, to turn out plays containing such and such ingredients in such and such proportion — as if the making of plays were one with the making of puddings or pills. And the actor's practical difficulty—once he forswears the ideal of a tame dramatist who will make him a play as his cook makes him puddings—is that he must act what he finds to act. Once in a while arises the actor-dramatist who, like Molière, continues in both crafts. There are modern instances; in America, William Gillette; in France, at this moment, Sacha Guitry. Their work is noticeable, if for nothing else (*And, Molière on his pedestal apart, it is often noticeable for a great deal else*), for the nice adjustment of the play's content to the actor's opportunity. Otherwise, it may be no more in the best plays than in the worst—if by 'best' is implied a rounded completeness—that the actor will be able to explore the sheer possibilities of his art as the theatre of the new illusion defines it. He could more often, strangely enough, find the occasion in plays in which the dramatist has himself been impatient of the form chosen and has surcharged it with thought or with feeling. It is, in fact, to the dramatist's experiments in the enlargement of his own art that the actor should look for the development of his.

One practical difficulty immediately arises. The theatre, as we know it, provides small opportunity for experiment of any sort. There is always the audience to be thought of, naturally not interested in the art's future, but expecting the entertainment offered to be both rounded and complete, however smooth, however bare with repetition the ways of it may be worn. In the event the public does have to put up with a good deal of experimenting. Playwrights and actors both are encouraged to give their 'prentice hands practice at its expense to an extent that must make musicians, for instance, disciplined to a hard technical training, simply green with envy. They profit—though Heaven knows the theatre does not—by the public's ignorance of an art which it sets out nevertheless to enjoy. A pity that there should be no more encouragement of true experimenting, by the art's masters, not its 'prentices. For, of all the arts, drama can live least in the light of theory. The dramatist may project his play in imagination pretty completely; the individual actor can at best say what he means his performance to be; few will be rash enough to forecast an exact result for any free and fruitful collaboration of a whole company of actors with the dramatist and among themselves.

We are back to our first admission that this final process of the putting of the play on the stage is a very incalculable thing. And incalculable it must to some extent remain if its chief aim is to be the endowing of the play with anything we are to call life; for the term will escape æsthetic definition. We must join company with the musical critic who, in similar case, disposed of all argument by saying, 'I know a good tune when I hear it.' But no one who—with critical faculties equipped against mere fraud—has seen a play brought fully and freely to life on the stage, will ever again mistake the sham thing for the real; or ever again, one would suppose, be content with the sham; or, it is to be hoped, ever again, knowing the difference between the two, begrudge the actor his full share in the credit of the life-giving process.

What, then, is the actor's case; what should he claim from the modern drama; what has he to offer? The dramatist's chief gain from the theatre of the new illusion and the conventions which belong to it, has been—at the price of some limitation of his power to project things in the doing—a great extension of resource in picturing things as they are. There was more need, as well as more scope, for physical action upon the older stage, even as there was for the spell-binding sway of verse. But by the new illusion the attention of an audience can be focussed upon the smallest details without either words or action being used to mark them, light, darkness, and silence can be made eloquent in themselves, a whole gamut of effectiveness has been added. It has brought new obligations—of accuracy, of sincerity, of verisimilitude in general, as we have noted. Then gain and loss both must be reflected in the actor's opportunity. His chances of doing are curtailed; in their stead new obligations of being are laid upon him. Can he not turn them to his profit?

One is tempted to imagine a play—to be written in desperate defiance of Aristotle—from which doing would be eliminated altogether, in which nothing but being would be left. The task set the actors of it would be to interest their audience in what the characters *were*, quite apart from anything they might *do;* to set up, that is to say, the relation by which all important human intimacies exist. If the art of the theatre could achieve this it would stand alone in a great achievement.

Plays of an approximate intention do indeed exist; but in England at least, they have never come to their own—even to such limited popularity as might be expected for them. There are reasons for this; the best being that the plays are mostly not English products. And while an English actor may reproduce the doings of a Frenchman or a Russian with sufficient fidelity, we cannot expect him to make real to us such an abstraction as his 'being.' So we have usually had the plays with the best part of them left out.

This opens up a line of inquiry worth pursuing for our present purpose. The dramatist must allow for the means of expression that come naturally to the people he is picturing. And expression is a racial thing. But when the influence of a technic of play construction spreads abroad, it is apt to affect plots, character-drawing and dialogue as well, everything but the actual language in which the derivative play may be written. For an instance, take the influence of French drama on English during the last century. We may rightly welcome for their good effect upon our native product French plays acted by Frenchmen, or even their translation; but a century's crowding of our theatre with adaptations has left the English drama

full of plots, situations, and figures that may—or
may not—have some relation to life in France, but in
England must rank as mechanism merely. The average
farcical comedy with its rooms with four doors *(French
rooms, as well as French stages, do as often as not have four
doors)*, peopled by distorted shadows from the world
of the French provinces and the half-world of Paris, the
grande dame, the *père noble,* the *raisonneur!* Now even
when an Englishman passes fifty and it grows hard to
stop him talking, he seldom becomes a *raisonneur.* The
word and the habit are equally French.

One result of all this, and not the least harmful, is that
Englishmen have come to be thought of as a race of
bad actors. Naturally they must seem so, when they
are encouraged to deny their race in the practice of
this most racial of all the arts. It is a nuisance for the
English dramatist, no doubt, that his countrymen do
not in the ordinary business—even in the extraordinary
moments—of life express themselves with fluency.
Well, it presents him with a difficulty he must learn to
surmount.

He can, of course, call convention to his help. But he
must honestly develop the convention and not try to
borrow one ready made. There lies one to his hand;
and the well-developed use of it might provide at least
a partial solution of our problem, might do much to
help the actor to his heritage again. Englishmen are
not glib, but the essential strength of poetic speech is
a tradition with them. By which one does not mean,
of course, that they lisp in numbers, or imply that
on formal occasions they cannot be academically
dull. But in the natural speech of the people there is
often that power of expression and concentration of
meaning which is the essence of poetry, even though
the form be prose. And great English writers, from
Shakespeare to Hardy, have known how to sublimate

it and make it memorable. The speech of the Wessex peasant is not Mr Hardy's invention, nor did Dickens conjure Sam Weller and Mr Peggotty out of the void. And for as forceful a passage as any in 'Cymbeline,' turn to the gaoler's philosophy of hanging and his 'O the charity of a penny cord!' Indeed, whether it be in form of verse or prose, Shakespeare *(Once he shook free of the fashionable affectations of his time and but for falling later into some affectations of his own)* did but take the common speech of the people of one class and another as material for his magic.

And this seems certain. All dramatic dialogue needs to have something of this particular quality of poetry in it. It must be dynamic speech. Poetry and drama are organically akin even when they seem sundered both by subject and method. They are notably alike in this, for instance, that they call for economy of effect. Consider how short is even the longest play in comparison with a novel. The mere words of many an excellent part could be written with a fine pen on a postcard. The literary man's failure at playwriting is due, nine times out of ten, to his dialogue being so obviously but a convenient means by which he tells his story and of no further value to the play; it is therefore of no value to the actor at all. If dialogue does not serve three purposes at least, to advance the story, to exhibit the one character and provoke the exhibition of another, it fails of its primary purpose, and the play will go floundering. Further, and most importantly, it must be charged with emotion. This lacking, the actor—unless he take matters so into his own hands that the play disappears in the process—is helpless.

And one may hazard an assertion that the modern dramatist's failure to provide due opportunity for his actors is oftenest this: he has discovered no sufficient substitute for the poetry and rhetoric in which lay the acting strength of the old plays. He may write excellent sense, and the audience, hearing it, will yet remain profoundly uninterested. Is the actor to blame? No; dramatic dialogue needs other qualities before it can be made to carry conviction. There is no solution, needless to say, in the dressing up of the play in poetic phrasing or the provision of a purple patch here and there. One must choose a medium and stick to it; only so can illusion be sustained. But the old dramatists did put into the hands—or, rather, into the mouths—of their actors a weapon of great, of magical power, by which, with little else to aid them, they could subdue their hearers to every illusion of a mimic world. Useless to-day to imitate its form, to fancy the strength lay in that. The essentials of it must be sought and somehow found. When found they are recognisable enough. Take any play and read two pages aloud. There can be no mistake. Tested by the living voice, either the language has life in it or it has not. A difficult medium, no doubt, to master, the prose of common speech which shall yet have the power of poetry. But it is what the actor asks if he is to command belief in his world of make-believe.

To put it in a phrase then; if the actor is to come to his own in the new drama, something the dynamic equivalent of poetry must be given to him as material for his share of the work. Nor is this too hard a saying. The dramatist's task—and the actor's coming after him—is the building up and exhibition of human character, the picturing of men's natures in the intimacies of their working. To this extent it is essentially a poet's task and the means to it are essentially those a poet seeks. A play's content may be what you will, matter for nothing but laughter; its dialogue may take any form whatever, from poetical imagery to the cracking of jokes. But it will be a good

play or a poor one, a living thing or dead, in so far
as we are brought to accept its inhabitants as fellow-
creatures or left indifferent to them. This is true of high
tragedy, and even the clown in the pantomime appeals
to some innocent knavery in our hearts that would find
it great fun to steal sausages, and to wield a red-hot
poker that was not too hot.

And magic is needed; the power of the spoken word
is a magic power. But the art of the theatre is not a
reasonable art. A play's dialogue is an incantation,
and the actors must bewitch us with it. They must
seem, now to be the commonest sort of folk, now
superhuman, and the form of their talk must fit them.
But, for all appearance, it must ever be of a trebly-
distilled strength. It must have this power of poetry in
it. It must be alive with more than the mere meaning
of words. In content and in form the modern dramatist
has much advanced his art. But still, too often, the
worthiest plays will leave us cold, respectful, when we
should be deeply moved, or paying them instead of
laughter a tolerant smile. What is wrong? This, for one
thing, I suggest. The dramatist of the new dispensation
has yet, as a rule, to learn both what to ask of his actors
and how best to help them to answer the demand.

www.ingramcontent.com/pod-product-compliance
Lightning Source LLC
Chambersburg PA
CBHW052107090426
42741CB00009B/1714